Why Does Cargo Spend Weeks in Sub-Saharan African Ports?

Why Does Cargo Spend Weeks in Sub-Saharan African Ports?

Lessons from Six Countries

Gaël Raballand, Salim Refas,
Monica Beuran, and Gözde Isik

THE WORLD BANK
Washington, D.C.

ISBN (paper): 978-0-8213-9499-1
ISBN (electronic): 978-0-8213-9500-4
DOI: 10.1596/978-0-8213-9499-1

Library of Congress Cataloging-in-Publication Data
Why does cargo spend weeks in Sub-Saharan African ports?: lessons from six case countries / by Gaël Raballand ... [et al.].
    p. cm.
Includes bibliographical references.
ISBN 978-0-8213-9499-1 — ISBN 978-0-8213-9500-4 (electronic)
  1. Freight and freightage—Africa, Sub-Saharan. 2. Shipping—Africa, Sub-Saharan. 3. Business logistics—Africa, Sub-Saharan. 4. Africa, Sub-Saharan—Commerce. I. Raballand, Gaël. II. World Bank.
  HE199.A357W49 2012
  387.1'640967—dc23

2012010815

Contents

Box

Figures

Tables

Foreword

Everyone agrees that Africa has a serious infrastructure deficit, estimated at about US$48 billion a year, and that this deficit is impeding the continent's competitiveness and hence its economic growth, to the tune of 1 or 2 percent of gross domestic product (GDP) per year. There is less agreement on how to solve the problem. Some advocate building more infrastructure while others suggest privatizing, or contracting out to the private sector, the management of infrastructure so that the discipline of the market will lead to more and better quality services.

This book graphically illustrates the problem in the case of Africa's ports. With the exception of Durban, cargo dwell times—the amount of time cargo spends in the port—average about 20 days in African ports, compared with 3 to 4 days in most other international ports. Yet neither of the solutions seems to be working. Adding additional berths has not brought down the dwell times. And with the exception of Durban and Mombasa, all major ports are already run by private container terminal operators.

The reason the solutions are not working—and this is the major contribution of this book—is that the long dwell times are in the interest of certain public and private actors in the system. Specifically, importers use the ports to store their goods; in Douala, for instance, storage in the port is the cheapest option for up to 22 days. Customs brokers, meanwhile, have little incentive to move the goods because they can pass on the costs of delay to the importers. Worse still, when the domestic market is a monopoly, the downstream producer has an incentive to keep the cargo dwell times long, as a way of deterring entry of other producers. The net result is inordinately long dwell times, ineffective interventions such as building more berths or privatizing the ports, and globally uncompetitive industries in African countries.

The case of cargo dwell times is an illustration of a more general problem in African development. Most, if not all, the binding constraints to growth, such as infrastructure, are the result of an equilibrium in which certain actors benefit from the existence of the constraint. Dealing with the proximate cause of the problem, such as the apparent lack of berths in the ports, is unlikely to trigger a solution. Rather, we need to understand the interests of the parties involved and look for ways of overcoming those interests in favor of the public's interest, which in this case is greater competitiveness and jobs. This is, of course, much more difficult than building berths or transferring ownership to the private sector. There are no clear-cut methods, but any approach requires that there be political support from the general public for reforms that will promote their interests. And before they offer their political support, the public needs to be informed. This book is a step in that direction.

Shantayanan Devarajan
Chief Economist
Africa Region
The World Bank

Acknowledgments

The main authors of this book are Gaël Raballand, Salim Refas, Monica Beuran, and Gözde Isik.

The book benefited from the input of John Arnold, Thomas Cantens, Pauline de Castelnau, Mohammed Hadi Mahihenni, Jean Kizito Kabanguka, Tshepo Kgare, Charles Kunaka, and Jean-François Marteau, and from the guidance of Shantanayan Devarajan, Supee Teravaninthorn, and Punam Chuhan-Pole.

Jean-François Arvis, Marc Juhel, Tomas Serebrisky, and Jan Hoffmann from the United Nations Conference on Trade and Development (UNCTAD) reviewed the book throughout the process.

Anca Dumitrescu, Enrique Fanta, Vivien Foster, Juan Gaviria, and Yonas Mchomvu provided comments on earlier drafts of the book.

Elizabeth Forsyth edited the book, and Ntombie Siwale and Shalonda Robinson supported the team.

The authors thank participants at the Tunis workshop held in December 2011, especially Mervin Chetty from Transnet and Marcellin Djeuwo from Cameroon customs, but also Rukia Shamte. They also thank TNS Sofres for conducting the firm surveys, especially Cédric de Smedt and Marco Pelluchi.

Finally, they thank the Bank Netherlands Partnership Program, especially Helena Nkole, for providing funding for half of the case studies, the Tunis workshop, and publication of the book.

Abbreviations

ASYCUDA	Automated System for Customs Data
CFS	container freight station
C&F	clearing and forwarding
CTOC	Container Terminal Operation Contract
DIS	destination inspection scheme
EDI	Electronic Data Interchange
FCFA	Franc Communauté Financière Africaine
FCVR	final classification and valuation report
GDP	gross domestic product
GPHA	Ghana Ports and Harbours Authority
GTAP	Global Trade Analysis Project
GUCE	Guichet Unique du Commerce Extérieur
IDF	import declaration form
ODCY	off-dock container yard
PIC	Port Improvement Committee
RTG	rubber-tired gantry
SAR	Special Administrative Region
SARS	South African Revenue Services
SSG	ship-to-shore gantry crane
TEU	20-foot equivalent unit

TICTS	Tanzania International Container Terminal Services
TISCAN	Tanzania Inspection Service Company
TLC	total logistics cost
TPA	Tanzania Ports Authority

CHAPTER 1

Introduction and Overview

Infrastructure gaps as well as high transport costs are critical factors hindering growth and poverty reduction in Sub-Saharan Africa. Although an efficient and low-cost transport system will not guarantee export success, it is a prerequisite for African countries to become competitive in the global market. As such, there has been renewed interest in understanding the nature of constraints that freight costs impose on trade, investment, and growth, especially in landlocked countries. Hummels and Schaur (2012) demonstrate empirically that longer transport time dramatically reduces trade. Without rapid import processes, trade based on assembling factories for exports is impossible, because delays and unpredictability increase inventories and prevent integration in global supply networks. Among 12 major impediments, the automotive industry in South Africa considers reducing inventories as the most important (Barloworld Logistics 2010). Without reducing the cost and improving the predictability of cargo dwell time (the time that cargo spends within the port or its extension), the objective of reducing inventories is not likely to be met.

In this regard, cargo dwell time in ports is critical. Arvis, Raballand, and Marteau (2010) demonstrate that more than half of the time needed to transport cargo from port to hinterland cities in landlocked countries in Sub-Saharan Africa is spent in ports.[1]

Over the past decade, the international donor community has been investing in projects that facilitate trade and improve trade logistics in the developing world. These projects have assumed incorrectly that customs, terminal operators, and other controlling agencies are solely responsible for the long delays in ports, with infrastructure coming in second.

In reality, customs responsibility (especially for months-long delays) may not be as important as usually perceived, and in-depth data collection and objective analysis are required to determine the actual drivers of long cargo delays. Such analysis has been lacking so far.

Study Objectives and Methodology

This study is timely because several investments are planned for container terminals in Sub-Saharan Africa. From a public policy perspective, disentangling the reasons behind cargo delays in ports is crucial to understanding (a) whether projects by the World Bank and other donors have addressed the most salient problems and (b) whether institutional port reform and infrastructure, sometimes complemented by customs reform, are the most appropriate approaches or should be adapted. Without such identification and quantification, projects may ultimately result in a limited impact, and structural problems of long delays will remain.

Port dwell time refers to the time that cargo (containers) spends within the port (or its extension).[2] This study disentangles cargo delays in ports using comprehensive analysis of original data sets. It uses three types of data:

1. Data collected in six ports in Sub-Saharan Africa: Tema (Ghana), Lomé (Togo), Douala (Cameroon), Mombasa (Kenya), Dar es Salaam (Tanzania), and Durban (South Africa)[3]
2. Firm surveys (manufacturers and retailers) conducted in Kenya, Nigeria,[4] South Africa, Uganda, and Zambia, to assess the extent of logistics constraints on importers and exporters, large- and small-scale companies, and traders and their demand for efficiency in ports
3. Information collected in discussions of results with stakeholders in the selected countries.

Ports were selected so as to have a representative sample of ports with regard to size, volume of traffic, and dwell time performance. Abidjan, Lagos, Tema, and Dakar ports account for more than two-thirds of total container traffic in West and Central Africa. Lomé handles smaller volumes of containers, but is perceived to have the shortest dwell time in West Africa, and it provides useful insights on the peculiarities of gateway ports with significant transit traffic. Douala, a medium-size port, is the largest port in Central Africa, handling about 150,000 TEUs (20-foot equivalent units) every year for both domestic and hinterland markets. Mombasa and Dar es Salaam are the largest ports in East Africa, with a capacity of about 400,000 TEUs, while Durban is the largest port in Sub-Saharan Africa.

Except for Durban and Mombasa, all of the ports studied are run by private container terminal operators, such as A. P. Møller (Maersk Group) and Bolloré for Douala and Tema, Bolloré for Lomé, and Hutchison Port Holdings, a subsidiary of the multinational conglomerate Hutchison Whampoa Limited, for Dar es Salaam.

Main Findings

Dwell time figures are a major commercial instrument used to attract cargo and generate revenues. Therefore, the incentives for a port authority and a container terminal operator are increasingly strong to lower the real figure to attract more cargo. At the same time, ports are more and more in competition, so the question of how to obtain independently verifiable dwell time data is increasingly critical to provide assurance that interventions are indeed having the intended effect.

In terms of indicators or targets for each port, average or mean dwell time has usually been the main indicator in Sub-Saharan Africa. It has the advantage of being both easy to compute and easy to understand. However, because a quarter of problematic shipments experience extremely long dwell time, average or mean dwell time can hardly decrease in the short and medium term. This has been the experience of Douala, for instance, which, at the end of the 1990s, sought to achieve an average dwell time of seven days, but still experiences an average dwell time of more than 18 days, despite improvements for some shippers.

Cargo dwell time in ports in Sub-Saharan Africa is abnormally long: more than two weeks on average compared to less than a week in the large ports in Asia, Europe, and Latin America (table 1.1). For benchmarking purposes, if we exclude Durban and, to a lesser extent, Mombasa, average dwell time in most ports in Sub-Saharan Africa is close to 20 days (compared to three to four days in most large international ports).

Another peculiarity in African ports is the frequent occurrence of very long dwell times, which adversely affect the efficiency of port operations and increase congestion in container terminals at a high cost to the

Table 1.1   Average Dwell Time in Sub-Saharan African Ports

Port	Average dwell time (number of days)
Durban	14
Douala	19
Lomé	18
Tema	20
Mombasa	11
Dar el Salaam	14
Average (excluding Durban)	16

Source: Kgare, Raballand, and Ittman 2011; firm surveys.

economy. Cargo dwell times in Sub-Saharan Africa also show an abnormal dispersion, with evidence that discretionary behaviors increase system inefficiencies and raise total logistics costs.

The private sector (terminal operator, customs broker, owner of container depots, and even shippers) does not seem to have an interest in reducing dwell time. In most ports in Sub-Saharan Africa, the interests of controlling agencies, port authorities, private terminal operators, logistics operators (freight forwarders), and large shippers collude at the expense of consumers. In many ports, there are strong incentives to use the port as a storage area. For example, storage in Douala port is the cheapest option for the first 22 days, which is 11 days more than the container terminal's free time. Firm surveys demonstrate that low logistics skills and cash constraints explain why most importers have no incentive to reduce cargo dwell time: in most cases, doing so would increase their input costs. Moreover, some terminal operators generate large revenues from storage, and customs brokers do not necessarily fight to reduce dwell time because time inefficiency is charged to the importer and eventually to the consumer.

Handling and operational dwell time add only two days (except in cases of severe congestion) to the average dwell time of 15 days and more. The bulk of the time pertains to transaction time and storage time, which result from the performance of controlling agencies and, even more important, from the strategies and behavior of importers and customs brokers. The strategies of importers can lead to use of the port as a cheap storage area, while collusion of interests among shippers, intermediaries, and controlling agencies may reinforce rent-seeking behaviors, to the detriment of cargo dwell time.

Market structure of the private sector explains the hysteresis of cargo dwell time. The structure of the African economies, which have few export-oriented producers and a preponderance of traditional import-export traders, reinforces the status quo, because they are rarely organized to be competitive worldwide. Based on firm surveys, it appears that companies may use long dwell times to prevent competition, like a predatory pricing mechanism, as well as to generate considerable rents.

In most ports in Sub-Saharan Africa, a vicious circle, in which long cargo dwell time (two to three weeks) benefits incumbent traders and importers as well as customs agents, terminal operators, or owners of warehouses, constitutes a strong barrier to entry for international traders and manufacturers (figure 1.1). This also explains why cargo dwell time has not decreased substantially for years: the market incentives are not strong enough in most cases, and importers can secure revenues by avoiding competition. This circle has been broken in Durban by the presence of a strong domestic private sector interested in global trade and public authorities willing to support them.

Weeks-long cargo dwell times in ports have become a serious obstacle to the successful integration of Sub-Saharan African economies into global trade networks, because they make lean, demand-driven manufacturing and trading activities virtually impossible.

Figure 1.1   The Vicious Circle of Cargo Dwell Time

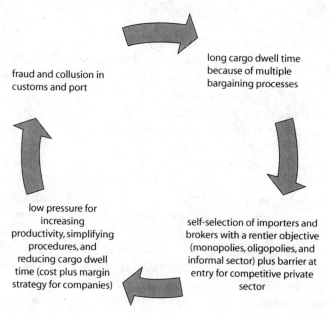

Source: Authors.

As a result, the widespread assumption that the provision of additional port infrastructure will necessarily translate into shorter dwell time does not hold in the medium to long term, especially when it comes to expanding existing ports. Using the example of Durban and simulations of container movements in a port terminal, we demonstrate that reducing dwell time from a week to four days more than doubles the capacity of the container terminal without any investments in physical extensions. Making investments in larger port storage areas is a suboptimal measure when efficiency gains can be obtained by speeding up clearance operations.

Implications for Donors in Sub-Saharan Africa

These findings could explain why many trade facilitation measures, such as community-based systems in ports, have been difficult to implement in Sub-Saharan Africa. Market incentives are too low for supply-side measures alone to bring about a radical improvement in trade logistics efficiency. Transparency is not welcomed because it is synonymous with the suppression of rents and promotion of competitive environments. The potential number of actors who may be drivers of change in the trading, industrial, and logistics sectors is much lower than generally anticipated because of risk-adverse behaviors.

Significant change is needed, including intervention of donors and development partners. Given the current level of dwell time in Sub-Saharan Africa, one of the worst options, which nevertheless is preferred in many instances, is to invest in additional storage and off-dock container yards (additional storage areas), where congestion and long cargo dwell times occur. Indeed, if dwell time is not reduced, after a couple of years, new dock yard extensions costing millions of U.S. dollars will be required, extensions that would be unnecessary if dwell time were reduced. Structural issues that lead to long dwell times, including the characteristics of demand, need to be tackled before undertaking costly physical extensions. If not, local populations will continue to pay twice for long dwell times: as taxpayers, because most physical extensions and infrastructure are expensive public investments, and as consumers, because inefficiencies and rents in the port are fully reflected in the final price of consumer goods and services. The construction of off-dock container yards in the outskirts of port cities, which relieve congestion in the transit port in the short run, also appear to be ill-advised from a system perspective. These additional storage areas tend to become rent-capture instruments in the hands of a few operators that charge high premiums on transit cargo and provide no added value. Such infrastructure was built in the 1970s and 1980s and abandoned in the 1990s, but is now back in fashion, as congestion has grown in some key ports.

The effective solutions to decrease dwell time in African ports will rely for the most part on the challenging task of breaking the private sector's collusive short-term strategies and providing adequate incentives for public authorities, intermediaries, and shippers to achieve optimal system equilibrium. Some possible dos and don'ts are presented in table 1.2.

Table 1.2   Possible Policy Recommendations

Dos	Don'ts
To deal with ports' capacity shortage, envisage a more optimal use of the existing capacity by targeting long-stay containers or cargo and encouraging fast clearance through price incentives	To deal with a ports' capacity shortage, immediately consider building additional capacity
Undertake a careful assessment of the way the private sector operates before investing in port infrastructure; understand demand before changing supply	Necessarily privatize or concession a container terminal to reduce dwell time
Inform public decision makers at very high level (prime minister, ministries of economy and finance) on the need to undertake public governance–related actions to build a broad coalition for change; thoroughly analyze the economic cost of poor system performance to the national economy	Support measures that create new rents and reduce system transparency such as the proliferation of off-dock container yards with no regulatory framework
Sensitize the local population and trading communities to the importance of port clearance performance and the proper calculation of total logistics costs	Consider as a given that everybody is aware that transport and port "costs" are high and address the issue of port delays only from a monetary cost perspective (with no mention of the time cost and reliability cost)
If a coalition can be built, design incentive tools, such as contractual relations between customs brokers and customs or between port operators and shippers; nurture good performance	Focus on poor performance, with no promotion of or reward for good permance
Undertake actions before arrival and after storage that directly and indirectly reduce dwell time, such as reinforcing incentives to clear shipments prior to arrivals and monitor and amend customs auction practices	Design information technology–only investment in a port or customs interface with no targeted actions to improve performance of the full cycle of transactions, including early and late processes in the clearance chain
Identify performance indicators, with a benchmark pegged to the most efficient shippers in the port	Report averages, with no distinct evaluation of good, average, and poor performance

Source: Authors.

Notes

1. Wilmsmeier, Hoffmann, and Sanchez (2006) find that the combined efficiency of the importing and exporting countries' ports has a very strong impact on maritime charges. Increasing the indicator of port efficiency by 1 percent reduces freight charges by 0.38 percent. If the two countries in the sample with the lowest port efficiency would improve their efficiency to the level of the two countries in the sample with the highest port efficiency, freight charges on the route between them would decrease an estimated 25.9 percent.

2. Even in Sub-Saharan Africa, more than half of total imports are containerized, and this traffic is growing. Data are more systematic and reliable for containers than for bulk traffic. We focus on import containers because they are important for import-export models and dwell time is usually low for outbound containers. Most boxes stay in port for one to two days to be marshaled before loading. Bulk or noncontainerized general cargo usually fits a specific pattern of storage and loading or unloading strategies.

3. This study selected the largest or among the largest ports in the four subregions of Africa: Durban in Southern Africa (which is also the largest in Sub-Saharan Africa), the two largest in East Africa (Mombasa and Dar es Salaam), Douala in Central Africa, and Lomé and Tema in West Africa.

4. Nigeria was selected because it undertook a major port reform but has continued to suffer from long dwell time. It is one of the most important African economies.

References

Arvis, Jean-François, Gaël Raballand, and Jean-François Marteau. 2010. *The Cost of Being Landlocked: Logistics Costs and Supply Chain Reliability.* Washington, DC: World Bank.

Barloworld Logistics. 2010. *Supply Chain Foresight, Growth in Adversity: Resilience and Recovery through Innovation.* Sandton, South Africa: Barloworld Logistics.

Hummels, David, and Georg Schaur. 2012. "Time as a Trade Barrier." NBER Working Paper 17758, National Bureau of Economic Research, Cambridge, MA. http://www.nber.org/papers/w17758.

Kgare, Tshepo, Gaël Raballand, and Hans W. Ittman. 2011. "Cargo Dwell Time in Durban." Policy Research Working Paper 5794, World Bank, Washington, DC.

Wilmsmeier, Gordon, Jan Hoffmann, and Ricardo Sanchez. 2006. "The Impact of Port Characteristics on International Maritime Transport Costs." In *Research in Transportation Economics,* vol. 16, ed. Kevin Cullinane and Wayne Talley. Amsterdam: Elsevier.

CHAPTER 2

Literature Findings and Methodological Considerations

This chapter presents both findings from the literature and methodological considerations from a worldwide perspective. Despite the paucity of research in this field for Sub-Saharan Africa, the findings from other countries are relevant to countries in the region. However, as demonstrated in this report, some specificities in Sub-Saharan Africa, such as abnormally long cargo dwell times, the dominance of the general trading model, a lack of competition in some sectors of the economy, and the importance of cash constraints, may weaken the incentive to move goods rapidly through the port.

Literature Findings

Cargo dwell time in ports has long been identified as a crucial operational issue of modern logistics. Back in 1978, a seminal report by the National Academy of Sciences in the United States noted, "The old saying 'time is money' is especially germane to modern port activity. The greatest saving in total cargo transport time can be made during the port transfer process, not the feeder or shipping transport segments" (National Academy of Sciences 1978, 90).

That report emphasized the importance of dwell time in port opera-tions, and its observations are still relevant today. For example, the report noted the adverse impact of long dwell times on total logistics costs: "It is necessary to reduce time spent in port by vessel and cargo to reduce shippers' total shipping costs" (National Academy of Sciences 1978, 103). It also rightly identified port dwell time as a crucial factor of com-petition between ports: "Timely service is the most important ingredient a port can offer to both importers and exporters" (National Academy of Sciences 1978, 95).

Port researchers have studied the issue of port dwell time by looking at four main topics: port operations and, in particular, the means of opti-mizing port productivity; trade competitiveness, which considers the impact of cargo dwell time on trade; port competition, which has recently been the subject of growing attention in the context of direct competition between port terminals at the regional and global levels; and supply chain performance, with authors such as Robinson (2002) calling for a paradigm shift to focus on the role of ports in global supply chains. Table 2.1 summarizes the main findings in the literature.

To our knowledge, no one has specifically analyzed port dwell time as a subject of research by itself. In other words, port dwell time is generally seen as a determinant of analytical outputs such as port efficiency, port capacity, or even trade volumes, but is not treated as an issue worthy of attention by itself. Nevertheless, research has shown its growing impor-tance and relevance in the context of modern port operations and trade logistics. This study intends to fill this gap in knowledge.

Port Operations

From an operational perspective, researchers are interested in the deter-minants of the operational performance of ports and the means and resources to optimize it. The primary indicators of operational perfor-mance are vessel turnaround time and port throughput. Asset perfor-mance indicators are also widely used to compare berth, yard, or gate performance of different ports. Cargo dwell time in terminals appears to be only a secondary indicator, since it depends on the characteristics of the cargo and the shipper (Chung 1993).

Few attempts have been made to model cargo dwell times in terminals as such, with the noticeable exception of Moini et al. (2010), who use data-mining algorithms to estimate dwell times for a U.S. container termi-nal. Vessel turnaround time, however, has been subject to many modeling attempts, the most traditional being queuing models that depend on three

Table 2.1 Summary of the Main Findings in the Literature on Cargo Dwell Time in Ports

Topic	Literature	Treatment of the dwell time issue
Operations	Moini et al. (2010)	Estimation of dwell time using data-mining techniques
	UNCTAD (1985), Frankel (1987), Dharmalingam (1987), Dally (1983)	Dwell time as a determinant of container yard capacity
	Huynh (2006)	Dwell time as a determinant of yard capacity and productivity
	Farrell (2009)	Two-way relationship between dwell time and throughput
Trade facilitation	Dasgupta (2009)	Dwell time as a barrier to trade
	Sengupta (2008)	Necessity for reforms
	Arvis, Raballand, and Marteau (2010)	Dwell time as a component of transaction costs; the effect on trade of uncertain dwell times
	Djankov, Freund, and Pham (2006)	Impact of dwell time on probability of trading with the United States
	USAID (2004)	Impact of dwell time on GDP and regional trade
	Hummels (2001)	Cost of time for international trade
	Nordås, Pinali, and Geloso Grosso (2006)	Cost of time for international trade and the importance of time in manufacturing and retail supply chains
Port competitiveness	Veldman and Bückmann (2003), Nir, Lin, and Liang (2003), De Langen (2007), Tongzon and Sawant (2007)	Dwell time as a determinant of port choice
Supply chain performance	Sanders, Verhaeghe, and Dekker (2005)	Dwell time as a determinant of port choice and trade generation
	UNCTAD (1985)	Long-term storage in ports and the issue of pricing
	Rodrigue and Notteboom (2009)	Terminals as extensions of distribution centers
	Nordås, Pinali, and Geloso Grosso (2006)	Modern supply chains as an essential ingredient for time-sensitive products
	Rodrigue and Notteboom (2009)	Ports as strategic storage units in international supply chains
	Wood et al. (2002)	Impact of lead time underestimates on dwell times

Source: Authors.

inputs: the distribution of arrivals, the distribution of service times, and the number of servers—that is, berth stations (Tsinker 2004). Vessel service times are an important component of cargo dwell time in congested ports, and it is therefore important to understand the dynamics of these queuing models, but for most ports, the bulk of cargo dwell time is spent in the yard, and vessel turnaround times are of secondary importance to shippers. However, cargo dwell time in terminals enters most operational port models not as an output, but as an explanatory variable.

Traditional attempts to design yard storage capacity—for example, from either a demand or a supply approach—use cargo dwell time as a main variable (box 2.1). In a more recent attempt, Huynh analyzes this relationship between dwell time and yard capacity by taking into account rehandling productivity and storage strategies (Huynh 2006). He concludes that port authorities should be well informed about the impact of dwell time on yard productivity before setting tariffs or free time periods that encourage long dwell times.

Box 2.1

Classic Formulas for Container Yard Storage Capacity as a Function of Dwell Time

Demand approach

$$CY = (C_p * A * DwT) * (1 + F)/360 \hspace{2cm} \text{(UNCTAD 1985)}$$
$$CY = [C_p * A * (Dwt + 2)]/[365 * Z * 10^4 * (H + 2h) * U] \hspace{1cm} \text{(Frankel 1987)}$$

Supply approach

$$C_C = GS_A * (0.6 * S) * (K/DwT) \hspace{2cm} \text{(Dharmalingam 1987)}$$
$$C_C = (GS_T * H * W * K)/(DwT * F), \hspace{2cm} \text{(Dally 1983)}$$

where CY is the required container yard, C_p is the projected container volume (20-foot equivalent unit, TEU), A is the area per container volume (TEU), DwT is the average dwell time in the container yard, F is the peaking factor, Z is the storage utilization factor, H is the average expected stack height by the average number of containers in used stacks, h is the standard deviation of stack height, U is the total area utilization, C_C is the container capacity (per year), GS_T is the total ground slot, GS_A is the available ground slot, S is the ground slot utilization factor, K is the number of days per year, and W is the number of working slots (in TEUs) in a container yard.

Source: Bichou 2009.

Port simulation models also take cargo dwell time as a variable. They consist generally of a set of modules with complex interaction and backward loops: an input module, a ship generator module, a ship operation module, a cargo-handling module, and a warehouse operation module (Hassan 1993). Dwell time is an input to the ship operation module and the warehouse operation module, and most recent techniques take into account the two-way relationship between dwell time and port capacity. This two-way relationship has been explored in analytical papers, such as Farrell (2009), albeit without an explicit analytical formulation of cargo dwell time as a model output.

Trade Competitiveness

Another research field where cargo dwell time has been given specific attention is international trade, specifically in the context of trade facilitation initiatives. However, the impact of long cargo dwell time on trade efficiency has only recently been seen as a major hindrance to the development of low-income countries. When analyzing key issues in India's international trade, Dasgupta identifies port logistics, specifically cargo dwell time, as the area most in need of reform (Dasgupta 2009, 239). Cargo dwell time also enters the equation of trade cost proposed by Sengupta in his book on the economics of trade facilitation (Sengupta 2008, 178). And achieving more time-efficient port clearance operations is often, perhaps always, a main objective of trade and transport facilitation projects that have been designed to address comprehensively the physical and other obstacles to trade in developing countries.

In addition to the long duration of container stays in the port, Arvis, Raballand, and Marteau (2010) identify the unpredictability of cargo dwell times as a major contributor to trade costs because shippers need to "compensate for the uncertainty by raising their inventory levels" (Arvis, Raballand, and Marteau 2010, 47). In other words, delay is not the only issue of importance when considering the impact of dwell time on the performance of trade; predictability and reliability of cargo dwell times are equally important because they have a major impact on the total costs of trade logistics.

Some modeling works have been instrumental in showing the direct impact of longer dwell times on trade. Djankov, Freund, and Pham (2006), for example, use a gravity model to calculate that each additional day that a product is delayed prior to being shipped reduces trade by at least 1 percent. In an attempt to show the broad economic impact of port inefficiency, Kent and Fox (2005) use a general equilibrium model to calculate the impact of port delays in the port of Puerto Limón, Costa Rica, on the regional economy of Central America (USAID 2004). They conclude that removing port inefficiencies, including long dwell times, would improve the gross domestic product (GDP) of Costa Rica by 0.5 percent.[1] Two major shortcomings of the general equilibrium model are the impossibility of separating containerized maritime trade from other modes and the robustness of the estimated inventory cost per day. In an earlier work that serves as reference on the matter, Hummels (2001) estimates that each additional day that cargo spends in transport (including port dwell time) reduces by 1–1.5 percent the probability that the United States will source from that country. And each day saved in shipping time is estimated to be worth 0.8 percent ad valorem for manufactured goods. Nordås, Pinali, and Geloso Grosso (2006) use comparable techniques to estimate trade flow probability as a function of lead time. They conclude that port efficiency is crucial to the successful integration of a country into the global trading system (Nordås, Pinali, and Geloso Grosso 2006, 36).

Port Competition

The container revolution started during the late 1950s in the United States. Two decades of international trade boom followed, leading to the development of modern container ports, especially in Western Europe and North America. As a result, port competition has attracted much scholarly attention in these regions, with a special focus on the "North Range" in Europe (ports of Antwerp, Bremen, Felixstowe, Hamburg, Le Havre, and Rotterdam) and the main U.S. ports (Chang and Lee 2007). At that time, global transport chains were still fragmented, uncoordinated, and inefficient. Competition was driven mainly by cost (Magala and Sammons 2008).

Later on, following the rise of powerful economies in East Asia and trade globalization, port competition shifted toward trade-offs between cost and quality of service. By the end of the 1990s, competition among modern container-based ports was at its peak (Chang and Lee 2007), and the top five container ports in the world were located in East Asia, principally China, following a short period of domination by ports in Japan, the Republic of Korea, and Taiwan, China, which had all invested heavily in port infrastructure to develop regional superhubs (Wang and Slack 2004). In other parts of the world, including North America, the same trends were evident, and container superhubs had developed in Northern

Europe (Antwerp, Hamburg, Rotterdam), Southern Europe (Algeciras, Gioia Tauro), the United States (Long Beach, Los Angeles, New York–New Jersey), and other markets (Dubai).

It is in this context that port dwell time started playing a crucial role in the competition between ports. Competition shifted from competition for lower cost to competition for faster, better, and more cost-effective access to international markets (Magala and Sammons 2008).

Because of this intense competition, various studies have highlighted the determinants of port choice and port competitiveness in contestable hinterlands.[2] Several of these studies identify cargo dwell time as a critical explanatory variable in port selection that enters the formulation of demand function (Veldman and Bückmann 2003; Nir, Lin, and Liang 2003; De Langen 2007; Tongzon and Sawant 2007; Sanders, Verhaeghe, and Dekker 2005). But since the objective of these models is usually to forecast traffic growth or market shares, there is little discussion of the actual importance of port dwell time for port clients. The techniques used tend to be "broad-brush" and "mechanistic" in nature, with "their success being judged by their predictive power rather than their explanatory ability" (Mangan, Lalwani, and Gardner 2002).

Supply Chain Management
The very focus of port management has changed radically in recent years with the advent of containerization and the "terminalization of supply." The objective of optimizing the use of port facilities has been gradually replaced by performance objectives that seek to gain competitive advantage over other ports. Since 1995, the United Nations Conference on Trade and Development (UNCTAD), for example, has recommended the implementation of performance-based yard tariffs that would encourage shippers to reduce the dwell time of containers in terminals. However, in many places, the promotion of efficient behavior among port users has met with resistance from shippers, who tend to use the terminal as a storage area—hence the difficulty of finding acceptable optimum levels of use. Specific pricing objectives have been proposed, but the implementation of effective storage tariffs is very complex (UNCTAD 1985).

Similarly, Rodrigue and Notteboom (2009) argue that freight forwarders use terminals as an extended component of their distribution centers and try to take full advantage of free time, while terminal operators try to restrict such behavior. Nordås, Pinali, and Geloso Grosso (2006) use a few case studies to show that a broader range of products are becoming time sensitive following the adoption of modern supply chain management practices in the manufacturing and retail sectors.

The functional use of terminals as a cheap storage area brings new challenges to terminal operating companies that are not limited to pricing issues. High dwell times are no longer indicators of poor terminal performance in general but, in some circumstances, are "perceived as an indicator of a higher level of integration between the port and inland freight distribution brought by supply chain management" (Rodrigue and Notteboom 2009). The objective of helping port users to achieve better supply chain performance would therefore lead terminal operating companies to accept or even support long cargo dwell times. Rodrigue and Notteboom conceptualize this paradigm shift from "bottleneck-derived terminalization," where the port terminal is essentially a source of delay and a capacity constraint in the shippers' supply chain, to "warehousing-derived terminalization," where the terminal replaces the warehousing facilities of shippers and gradually becomes a strategic storage unit (Rodrigue and Notteboom 2009).

Such a functional shift comes with a few prerequisites: extra terminal capacity (low occupancy rates), modern supply chain practices (such as integration and synchronization of supply and demand or just-in-time manufacturing), and good liner shipping connectivity, which is indispensable for responsive supply chains. These assumptions would probably not hold in most Sub-Saharan African countries today: liner shipping connectivity is very low, with most countries being in the lowest tier of the UNCTAD liner shipping connectivity ranking (UNCTAD 2009),[3] most container terminals have occupancy rates higher than 80 percent, and supply chain maturity is at an early stage, with a dominance of producer-driven supply chains based on cost-efficiency rather than responsiveness.

The use of terminals as warehouses is nevertheless prominent in African ports, as is demonstrated in this report. In fact, no attempt has been made to model the demand of shippers for long-term storage in a way that is applicable to ports in Sub-Saharan Africa. Yet the problem has been identified for a long time: "As far as they are interested in warehousing, shippers are biased in favor of utilizing the port facility as much as possible" (UNCTAD 1985). They tend to have negative perceptions about the reliability of shipping services and "build delay time into their production planning" to cater to the worst situation. If the container happens to arrive on time, shippers delay the shipment until they need it (Wood et al. 2002, 169).

Methodological Considerations

The time a container spends in port can be divided into three segments: entry, storage, and exit. For inbound containers, these segments refer to the times spent on the following:

1. Unloading the vessel and transferring containers to the storage yard, t_1
2. Waiting in the container yard, t_2
3. Processing the container out of the port, t_3.

The time spent undertaking the physical transfer—activities 1 and 3—depends primarily on the efficiency of the terminal operator. The time spent waiting in the container yard depends on the time spent completing the various procedures associated with clearing import cargo, completing an intermodal transfer, and arranging for the inland transfer. For ports with off-dock container yards (ODCYs), additional time is required to transfer the containers from the port to the ODCY, t_4. As a result, the average dwell time for a port alone is $t_1+t_2+t_3$. But for the containers, it is $t_1+(1-\alpha)(t_2+t_3) + \alpha(t'_2+t'_3+t_4)$, where α is the proportion of containers going to the ODCY and t'_2 and t'_3 are the average times for activities 2 and 3 in the ODCY.

Factors to Be Modeled While Looking at Dwell Time

For individual shippers, the length of port dwell time is determined by three factors: the efficiency of container-handling operations, the complexity of the transactions for border control and intermodal exchange, and the requirements of the consignees for storing cargo in the port. The basic cargo-handling operations in a container terminal are the movements of goods across the berth, in and out of the storage area, and entering and exiting the port from the landside. The efficiency of these operations affects the time and costs of the transfer. Each operation has capacity constraints, and delays occur more frequently as the level of use approaches this capacity. Both the port and the terminal operator are responsible for the efficiency of these operations.

Transactions are associated with the intermodal transfer of cargo across a border. They include the procedures of customs and other border agencies that control the type and quality of goods entering and exiting a country. They also include the financial transactions associated with the transfer of ownership and liability for the cargo as well as with the collection of duties and taxes on it. In the case of imports, the transfer of ownership involves exchanging the bill of lading between the shipping line and the consignee. The transfer of liability between the shipping line, port operator, and provider of land transport involves the exchange of documents for receipt and delivery of the cargo. The minimum time required to complete these transactions is determined by parties other than the cargo owner; however, the actual time is determined by the efforts of cargo owners and their agents to coordinate with these parties and to cooperate in completing the transactions.

The decision of the consignee to store cargo in the port rather than elsewhere along the supply chain is based on cost and convenience. The period of storage depends on the delivery time as well as on the cost of alternative storage outside the port. The use of port storage therefore depends on its pricing and the amount of duties and taxes payable when cargo leaves the port.

Current Policy Orientations

The primary focus of policy makers has been on costs, and there is growing awareness of the need to equip least developed countries with efficient transport networks, including modern ports. The private sector has been called upon largely to operate and manage these new facilities. The impact of these investments has been subject to increasing attention, and operating costs or productivity measures have been monitored closely.

In parallel, global trade negotiations have progressively raised the issue of trade facilitation as a critical component of the economic development of poor nations. The focus has been on simplification and transparency of border-crossing procedures, and vast programs have been undertaken to modernize customs administrations.

Finally, logistics performance has recently been given attention as part of global benchmarking initiatives to evaluate the ease of doing business in different countries, and the efficiency of logistics and transport services is increasingly considered a major contributor to high import costs and long delays.

What seems to be missing in the body of knowledge about barriers to international trade in developing countries is analysis of the business strategies of market players. The competitive context in these countries is such that market inefficiencies are many, and suppliers or users can therefore take advantage of the situation to increase their revenues to the detriment of the final users.

Although studying infrastructure stock and productivity, border-crossing procedures, logistics performance, and private sector strategies is useful, our primary focus in the case studies presented in this report is on private sector strategies. In particular, the focus is on shippers, terminal operating companies, and logistics providers. Other approaches are also needed in order to document the success or failure of recent reforms and investments and to complement the formulation of policy recommendations.

Disaggregated Analysis

The parallel clearance formalities undertaken by shippers can be classified into three main constituents of dwell time in ports:

- *Operational dwell time*, which refers to the performance of physical operations
- *Transactional dwell time*, which refers to the performance of clearance formalities
- *Storage dwell time*, which refers to the voluntary storage of cargo in the container yard as part of a wider inventory management strategy.

The importance of each component of total dwell time needs to be analyzed with regard to the context. The interrelationships between them are also of critical importance because high correlations tend to support the existence of behavioral determinants of long dwell time.

Operational dwell time is evaluated in this report using extensive shipment-level data and performance indicators that are generally collected by terminal operating companies. Customs administrations have implemented electronic procedures that allow for close monitoring of the efficiency of the border-crossing process as a proxy for transactional dwell time. The cargo-tracking instruments used by carrying and forwarding operators and shippers are instrumental in gaining insight on typical statistics and strategies for storage and overall dwell time.

Establishment of a Demand Model. The bulk of cargo dwell time (up to 90 percent) is spent in the storage areas of the terminal or the ODCY. To interpret (long) cargo delays in ports requires understanding the determinants of yard storage times. This analysis is performed at two levels:

- At the supply level, by looking at the performance and organization of terminal operating companies and intermediaries, such as logistics providers or customs brokers, and the processes established by public authorities in the import process
- At the demand level, by modeling the behavior of shippers with regard to port storage.

The general framework of the research problem is depicted in figure 2.1. A system of players is involved in a set of commercial or administrative transactions that are performed to allow containerized goods to enter the country. Each player in the system operates in a specific competitive context and within a given set of constraints and incentives. Analysis is necessary to gain insight into the decision-making process of all these players, their efficiency, and the interactions between different players that can explain the reason for long cargo dwell times.

This analytical work was complemented by field investigations with three main objectives:

- *Data collection.* The analytical models are data intensive, and parameters were defined or updated using the latest available data.
- *Qualitative analysis.* Qualitative analysis was undertaken to refine assumptions of the model, identify new ways of approaching the problem, and eventually distinguish between conclusions that are applicable at a regional level and those that are specific to each country.
- *Evaluation of clearance procedures.* Physical port clearance is clearly affected by the inefficiencies of clearance transactions, and the interdependencies between both processes were sounded out. In particular, we sought to identify those formalities or processes that have a substantial impact on cargo dwell time.

Having presented the main findings of the literature and an analytical framework in this chapter, the next chapter presents the main

Figure 2.1   Port System Model for Container Imports

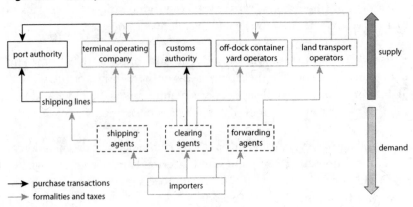

Source: Authors.

findings of the case studies undertaken within the framework of this study.

Notes

1. Port efficiency is computed through the parameter *ams* of the Global Trade Analysis Project (GTAP) model, which is a computable general equilibrium model of the world economy. The port of Puerto Limón (Costa Rica) has an excess delay of 13.5 hours as compared to the port of Cartagena (Colombia), and additional costs of US$18 per 20-foot equivalent unit (TEU) are incurred, mainly because of vessel costs. Kent and Fox (2005) use Hummel's inventory cost estimate (0.8 percent per day) and an average cargo value of US$26,919. The formula for parameter *ams*, which simulates an additional tariff on goods, is $t = (13.5/24) \times 0.8 + (US\$18/26,919 \times 100) = 0.517$. The higher cargo dwell times in the port of Puerto Limón are therefore equivalent to an additional tariff of 0.517 percent on manufactured cargo, which exerts a drag on the national economy. The aggregate impact simulated through the GTAP model is 0.5 percent of GDP.

2. These models are only applicable to contestable hinterlands, where the competitive advantage of container terminals determines market share. In Sub-Saharan African countries, most gateway ports operate with a vast captive hinterland and have no need to compete over time or cost to attract traffic.

3. With the exception of South Africa, which is ranked thirty-second.

References

Arvis, Jean-François, Gaël Raballand, and Jean-François Marteau. 2010. *The Cost of Being Landlocked: Logistics Costs and Supply Chain Reliability.* Washington, DC: World Bank.

Bichou, Khalid. 2009. *Port Operations, Planning, and Logistics.* London: Informa.

Chang, Young-Tae, and Paul T. W. Lee. 2007. "Overview of Interport Competition: Issues and Methods." *Journal of International Logistics and Trade* 99 (5): 99–121.

Chung, Kek Choo. 1993. "Port Performance Indicators." Infrastructure Note PS-6, Transportation, Water, and Urban Development Department, World Bank, Washington, DC. http://siteresources.worldbank.org/INTTRANSPORT/Resources/336291-1119275973157/td-ps6.pdf.

Dally, H. K. 1983. *Container Handling and Transport: A Manual of Current Practice.* London: Cargo Systems IIR Publications.

Dasgupta, Partha, ed. 2009. *The WTO at the Crossroads.* New Delhi: Concept Publishing.

De Langen, P. W. 2007. "Port Competition and Selection in Contestable Hinterlands: The Case of Austria." *European Journal of Transport and Infrastructure Research* 7 (1): 1–14.

Dharmalingam, K. 1987. *Design of Storage Facilities for Containers: A Case Study of Port Louis Harbour.* Mauritius: Ports and Harbors.

Djankov, Simeon, Caroline Freund, and Cong Pham. 2006. "Trading on Time." Policy Research Working Paper 3909, World Bank, Washington, DC.

Farrell, Sheila. 2009. "Factors Influencing Port Efficiency: A Case Study of Dar es Salaam." Paper presented at a conference of the International Association of Maritime Economics, Copenhagen, June 24–26.

Frankel, E. G. 1987. *Port Planning and Development.* New York: John Wiley and Sons.

Hassan, Said A. 1993. "Port Activity Simulation: An Overview." *Simulation Digest* 23 (2): 17–36.

Hummels, David. 2001. "Time as a Trade Barrier." GTAP Working Paper 1152, Center for Global Trade Analysis, Department of Agricultural Economics, Purdue University, West Lafayette, IN.

Huynh, Nathan. 2006. "Boosting Marine Container Terminals Throughput: A Survey of Strategies." Paper 06-2744, presented at the annual meeting of the Transportation Research Board, Washington, DC, January.

Kent, Paul E., and Alan Fox. 2005. "The Broad Economic Impact of Port Inefficiency: A Comparative Study of Two Ports." Report by Nathan Associates for the U.S. Agency for International Development, Washington, DC. www .tcb-project.com.

Magala, Mateus, and Adrian Sammons. 2008. "A New Approach to Port Choice Modeling." *Maritime Economics and Logistics* 10 (1–2): 9–34.

Mangan, John, Chandra Lalwani, and Bernard Gardner. 2002. "Modelling Port/ Ferry Choice in RoRo Freight Transportation." *International Journal of Transport Management* 1 (1): 15–28.

Moini, Nadereh, Maria Boilé, William Laventhal, and Sotirios Theofanis. 2010. "A Model to Estimate Container Dwell Time Using a Set of Determinants." Paper presented at the 89th annual meeting of the Transportation Research Board, National Research Council, Washington, DC.

National Academy of Sciences. 1978. "Case Studies on Maritime Innovation." Maritime Transportation Research Board, National Research Council, Washington, DC.

Nir, A.-S., K. Lin, and G-S Liang. 2003. "Port Choice Behaviour: From the Perspective of the Shipper." *Maritime Policy and Management* 30 (2): 165–73.

Nordås, Hildegunn Kyvik, Enrico Pinali, and Massimo Geloso Grosso. 2006. "Logistics and Time as a Trade Barrier." Trade Policy Working Paper 35, Organisation for Economic Co-operation and Development, Paris.

Robinson, Ross. 2002. "Ports as Elements in Value-Driven Chain Systems: The New Paradigm." *Maritime Policy and Management* 29 (3): 3–8.

Rodrigue, Jean-Paul, and Theo Notteboom. 2009. "The Terminalization of Supply Chains: Reassessing Port-Hinterland Logistical Relationships." *Maritime Policy and Management* 36 (2): 165–83.

Sanders, F. M., R. J. Verhaeghe, and S. Dekker. 2005. "Investment Dynamics for a Congested Transport Network with Competition: Application to Port Planning." Paper presented at the 23rd international conference of the System Dynamics Society, July 17–21, Boston. http://www.systemdynamics.org.

Sengupta, Nirmal. 2008. *The Economics of Trade Facilitation.* Oxford: Oxford University Press.

Tongzon, Jose L., and Lavina Sawant. 2007. "Port Choice in a Competitive Environment: From the Shipping Lines' Perspective." *Applied Economics* 39 (4): 477–92.

Tsinker, Gregory P. 2004. *Port Engineering: Planning, Construction, Maintenance, and Security.* Hoboken, NJ: John Wiley and Sons.

UNCTAD (United Nations Conference on Trade and Development). 1985. *Port Development: A Handbook for Planners in Developing Countries.* TD/B/C.4/175/rev. 1. New York: UNCTAD.

———. 2009. *Review of Maritime Transport.* New York: UNCTAD Secretariat. www.unctad.org.

USAID (U.S. Agency for International Development). 2004. *The Broad Economic Impact of Port Inefficiency: A Comparative Study of Two Ports.* Washington, DC: USAID. http://pdf.usaid.gov/pdf_docs/PNADC612.pdf.

Veldman, Simme J., and Ewout H. Bückmann. 2003. "A Model on Container Port Competition: An Application for the West European Container Hub-Ports." *Maritime Economics and Logistics* 5: 3–22.

Wang, James J., and Brian Slack. 2004. "Regional Governance of Port Development in China: A Case Study of Shanghai International Shipping Center." *Maritime Policy and Management* 31 (4): 357–73.

Wood, Donald F., Anthony P. Barone, Paul R. Murphy, and Daniel L. Wardlow. 2002. *International Logistics,* 2nd ed. San Francisco: AMACOM Books.

CHAPTER 3

Main Findings from the Case Studies

This chapter presents data on cargo dwell time in the six ports studied—Dar es Salaam, Douala, Durban, Lomé, Mombasa, and Tema—and strives to explain the main causes of delays.[1] It demonstrates that long dwell times are the norm in Sub-Saharan Africa. Moreover, despite numerous contributing factors, storage is the most important in most cases. The chapter is divided into two types of case studies: the first type gives benchmark figures, while the second type provides shipment-level analysis for Dar es Salaam and Douala and, therefore, is more useful than the usual analyses for understanding the main issues in this regard.

Dwell Time Benchmarks

In terms of performance, Durban appears to be a good benchmark for South African ports and, even more important, for Sub-Saharan African ports. Durban has by far the lowest cargo dwell time in Southern Africa and in Sub-Saharan Africa in general. Durban's dwell time is comparable to that of most ports in Europe or Asia, where dwell times of three to four days are the norm.

In Sub-Saharan Africa, dwell time in ports like Mombasa or Dar es Salaam is between 10 and 12 days, and, in the other major ports, it is longer than 15 days. Sub-Saharan African ports are unique in this regard.

When cargo dwell time is broken into operational, transactional, and storage dwell time,[2] Durban compares favorably with Mombasa and even more so with Douala on each factor (table 3.1). Storage plays a major role and is therefore discussed in chapter 4.

In these three ports, a significant amount of dwell time is attributable to transactional factors and storage. Although operational, transactional, and storage factors are common across the three ports, they differ in their impact on dwell time and cargo delays.

Moreover, dwell time depends mainly on the actions of importers, brokers, banks, and preshipment agencies: in Douala, all of them account for 13.5 days (70 percent of total time), whereas customs procedures account for 3 percent of total time, according to customs data. The share can be even higher if a customs agent and a broker take time to bargain (Djeuwo 2011).

Although operational dwell time is not the main factor explaining cargo dwell time, the condition of yard equipment does have an impact (limited to a few days). If equipment is in short supply or poorly maintained, this can reduce productivity and lead to yard congestion. This situation is particularly common in Dar es Salaam and Mombasa, where yard congestion is a recurrent problem.

Case Studies

This section presents cargo dwell time for the ports of Durban, Mombasa, Tema, and Lomé.

Table 3.1   Average Cargo Dwell Time in Durban, Mombasa, and Douala Ports

Dwell time factor	Durban		Mombasa		Douala	
	Number of days	Ratio of days to benchmarks	Number of days	Ratio of days to benchmark	Number of days	Ratio of days to benchmark
Operational	2	1.0	5	2.5	5	2.5
Transactional	1	1.0	3	3.0	5	5.0
Storage	1	1.0	3	3.0	9	9.0
Total dwell time	4	1.0	11	2.7	19	4.7

Source: Authors.

Durban

Durban enjoys unparalleled dominance in Sub-Saharan Africa with regard to both size and performance, but Transnet Port Terminal's aspiration to make Durban globally competitive means that the port is expected to meet the standards of other international ports, such as those of Rotterdam, Singapore, and others. Durban port shows that cargo dwell time is mainly a function of the characteristics of the private sector, but the onus is on public sector players, such as customs officials and the port authority, to put pressure on private sector users to comply with the rules and reduce cargo dwell time. It is still possible to reduce cargo dwell time in Durban, although this would be more difficult than it was in the early 2000s.

Data obtained for the Durban Container Terminal indicates an average of three to four days of dwell time since 2006. Figure 3.1 shows that the average dwell time at the port is less than four days for both imports and exports, with a slight peak of five to seven days around May 2010, which correlates with a strike at the port.

Dwell time for transshipments is around five to 10 days, with a few irregular peaks at around the 15-day mark, notably between July and September.[3] This is also related to the fact that "free time"[4] for transshipment is set at seven days instead of three (with low charges for stays shorter than 15 days).

Cargo is generally moved from the terminal to bonded warehouses before the free storage period of three days expires. The information provided, therefore, does not capture all dwell time figures for the port.

Figure 3.1   Dwell Time at Durban Container Terminal Pier 2, 2006–10

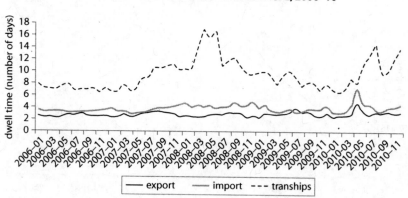

Source: Data provided by Transnet Port Terminal.

Additional data were also collected from agents handling cargo during the period from January to December 2010. According to owners of the main shipping lines and warehouses, less than 10 percent of containers go beyond the three-day period and less than 1 percent go beyond 28 days. Based on multiple interviews, it is possible to reconstruct dwell time frequency (see figure 3.2).

Mombasa

In the port of Mombasa, the average dwell time in 2007 was about 13 days, implying about five days of discretionary time.

While the reported average dwell time at the end of 2008 was about nine days, when the off-dock container yard (ODCY) boxes were included, this was closer to 11 days. Similarly, at the end of 2009, the reported average dwell time was six days, but when the ODCY containers were included, the average was closer to nine days. Although less dramatic than suggested in the port statistics, the reduction in dwell time was still significant.

The decline reported by the Kenya Ports Authority was consistent with the observations of the shipping lines and ODCY operators. One shipping line interviewed indicated that the decline in dwell time for the combination of transit and domestic imports leveled off at about 7.5 days.

The decline in dwell time after 2007 was significant for both domestic imports and transit imports: the average time spent in port was 12.5 and

Figure 3.2   Cargo Dwell Time Frequency in Durban Port

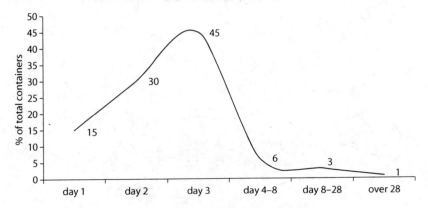

Source: Interviews with Transnet Port Terminal and with major shipping lines and warehouses.

14.8 days for domestic and transit imports, respectively. This implies a reduction of nearly eight days for transit cargo and about five days for imports. The reduction for domestic imports was due primarily to the reduction in congestion, as simpler procedures for processing documents probably saved one or two days.

The downward trend was attributable to three main factors: (a) improvement in cargo clearance procedures, (b) increase in storage tariffs, and (c) improvement in inland transportation, which allowed cargo to move more easily through and out of the port.

Tema

Average dwell time in Tema is around 20 days and remains rather stable. Few structural impediments exist to explain the relatively long dwell time for containers unloaded in the port of Tema. Berth productivity is reasonable for the region, and the time spent unloading does not contribute significantly to dwell time.

Although the regulatory procedures—in particular, cargo clearance activities—are unnecessarily complex and cumbersome given the level of technology employed, this does not have a significant impact on dwell time because it is possible to approve the valuation and classification of cargo prior to its arrival. As a result, most importers can complete clearance procedures within four to five days after arrival. It is reasonable to expect most containers to be cleared within a period of three to eight days.[5]

In contrast to these numbers, Meridian Port Services reported for 2009 that the average dwell time was 16.7 days for import containers, 21.3 days for inbound transit containers, 4.2 days for loaded export containers, and 6.1 days for empty outbound containers. The average for the combination of import and transit containers was 17.2 days, about 11 days more than the estimated processing time.

The slow decline in average dwell time reported by the port of Tema appears to have had a small impact on long-stay cargo. This is normal because containers do not stay in port because of normal clearance procedures or problems related to documentation and cash flow. Much of the very long-stay cargo is abandoned and must eventually be removed through customs seizure. Customs requires shipping lines to send a list of uncleared containers that have been in port more than 21 days. Customs then declares the cargo as long stay, but no specific rules govern when the content of these containers must be declared unclaimed and auctioned. Customs is often reluctant to go through the auction procedure, which is time-consuming and frequently gives rise to accusations of malfeasance.[6]

Lomé

The port of Lomé is an important hub for West and Central African maritime transport flows. With its natural draft of 14 meters, it is the only genuine deep-sea port in the subregion, ideally located at the heart of West African shipping networks. Regular calls are composed of both mother ships for east-west routes and feeder vessels for the region.

Container traffic has increased fourfold or fivefold since stevedoring activities were privatized in 2001; as a consequence, the port has reached the limit of its container-handling capacity. Two major projects to increase capacity are under way: the construction of a new pier dedicated to container traffic and the construction of a new port with a capacity of 1.5 million TEUs (20-foot equivalent units). Lomé cannot rely on a large domestic market, contrary to Tema, which benefits from Ghanaian traffic, Abidjan, which benefits from Côte d'Ivoire traffic, and Cotonou, which benefits from Benin traffic, though to a lesser extent (table 3.2 presents free time for select ports). Therefore, Lomé offers exceptionally long free time for traffic in transit.

Cargo in transit represents about half of the volume of container traffic in Lomé, as shown in figure 3.3. Procedures for containers in transit are similar to those for domestic traffic, with the noticeable difference that transiting cargo benefits from a longer free time period.

The downside is that this policy provides shippers with an incentive to use the port as a storage area and therefore has a significant impact on dwell time. A comprehensive data analysis demonstrates that only one-fourth of container imports are cleared in seven days or less, and the average port dwell time is 18 days in Lomé, which is comparable to other ports in the subregion. Figure 3.4 presents the distribution of container imports per dwell time interval.

Table 3.2   Free Time in Selected Ports

Port	Amount of free time (number of days)
Durban	3
Douala	11
Lomé (transit)	21
Hong Kong SAR, China	5

Source: Data provided by port authorities.

Figure 3.3   Container Traffic in Lomé Port, by Type of Cargo

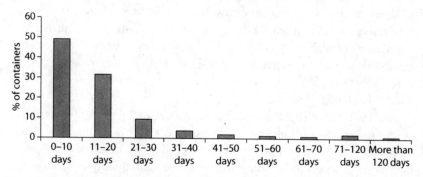

Source: Data provided by the Autonomous Port of Lomé.

Figure 3.4   Dwell Time for Container Imports in Lomé Port, 2009

Source: Data provided by the Autonomous Port of Lomé.
Note: Port authorities contest these figures and give lower dwell times because containers are dropped from statistics when they exit the yard. Comprehensive and reliable statistics in Lomé are not published transparently or regularly, contrary to all of the other ports studied, except Tema.

The following are the main components of delay in Lomé:

- Delay between vessel arrival and exchange of bill of lading
- Delay between the lodging of customs declaration and payment of fees
- Delay between the issue of delivery note and exit from port.

The stakeholders differ in each case. The first cause of delay is attributable to shipping lines and customs administration, the second, to customs brokers and customs administration, and the third, to customs brokers and container-handling companies. No prearrival clearance is possible at this time, which is a major obstacle to efforts to reduce cargo dwell time.

Shipment-Level Case Studies

The next two case studies present shipment-level analysis for the ports of Dar es Salaam and Douala. Analysis is based on several thousand observations over several months. It demonstrates the importance of various factors to explain long cargo dwell time, such as low volume, high value density, high fiscal pressure, and market concentration of clearing and forwarding (C&F) agents. These factors are applicable to the other ports studied, with the exception of Durban.

Dar es Salaam

The continuous growth in traffic since 2000, combined with an increase in dwell time, has caused a steady increase in the average number of containers stored in the container yard of Tanzania International Container Terminal Services (TICTS),[7] leading eventually to severe congestion. Prior to the increase in capacity in 2009, long dwell time for containers was the major factor determining high occupancy in the TICTS container yard.

Although it is difficult to estimate annual container-handling capacity precisely because of the subjective nature of operational indicators, such as number of berths, number of storage slots, or handling times, and because of the tight relation between capacity and quality of service, the container terminal in Dar es Salaam was expected to handle up to 250,000 containers a year when the concession was awarded in 2000.

Some additional equipment has been purchased since, and the total capacity has probably increased 10–30 percent. This increase in capacity has been far from sufficient, and the TICTS operator is unable to cope with the ever-increasing amount of container traffic, which reached close to 350,000 containers a year in 2008 (figure 3.5).

This traffic was equivalent to more than a million tons of imported goods in 2008. Table 3.3 shows the volume and destination of these imports for one quarter of that year and the relative distribution by country of destination. Local imports are by far the most important category, and the Democratic Republic of Congo, Rwanda, and Zambia are the primary destinations of transiting goods. The port of Dar es Salaam is a significant

Figure 3.5   Volume of Traffic and Terminal Capacity in Dar es Salaam Port, 2000–07

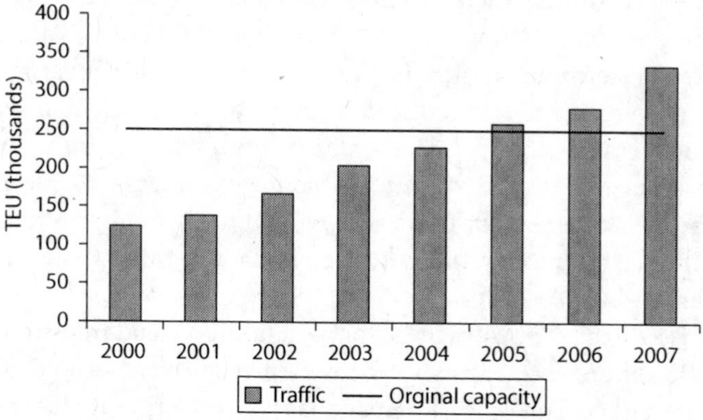

Source: Farrell 2009.

Table 3.3   Volume of Containerized Imports in Dar es Salaam Port, by Final Destination, September to November 2008

Final destination	Tons	% of containers
Domestic	302,840	71.9
Transit	118,220	28.1
Congo, Dem. Rep.	50,060	11.9
Zambia	27,600	6.6
Rwanda	21,000	5.0
Burundi	14,880	3.5
Uganda	2,760	0.7
Malawi	1,780	0.4
Kenya	100	< 0.1
Total	421,060	100

Source: Dar es Salaam Port data for 2008.

gateway for a wide region comprising, in particular, Burundi, eastern Democratic Republic of Congo, northern Zambia, and Rwanda, but its market share for each of these destinations remains low, as it apparently does not constitute a serious competitor to the main Kenyan, Mozambican, or South African ports, despite its favorable geographic position.

Dwell time for both imports and exports declined during the initial years of the concession and then rose, especially during 2008–09, before declining again to 14 days in 2011. Although the average dwell time for import containers was about 18 days in 2009, more than a third left the port within seven days.

In 2008, a specialized committee to address the problem of high dwell time—the Port Improvement Committee—was created under the impetus of the president of Tanzania. An important measure was to change the container terminal tariffs. In August 2009, storage charges were doubled, and free time was reduced from 10 to seven calendar days for imports but remained at 15 calendar days for transit cargo. Subsequently, a late clearance fee was introduced to encourage consignees to clear cargo within the free time period. This was intended to encourage importers to remove their cargo more rapidly, but the impact of this measure is difficult to determine.

There is a large set of consignees for both domestic and transit markets, with 2,205 different consignees for the domestic market and 1,351 for the transit market. The bulk of demand is from traders, but all other sectors (pharmaceutical industry, construction industry, public sector) are also represented.

Data collected show that 352 clearing agents handled local cargo clearance operations for more than 2,200 consignees over the period considered. This means that each clearing agent works, on average, for only six or seven consignees. At the same time, 95 clearing agents cleared goods for transit markets for 1,351 different consignees. On average, a clearing agent therefore works for 14 clients, which means that the clearing market is more concentrated for goods in transit than for local cargo.

If we look in more detail into clearing market concentration, more than 50 percent of the clearing market for goods in transit is in the hands of the seven top clearing agents, and 80 percent of the market is in the hands of the top 20. The 75 other clearing agents only handle marginal volumes. In general, clearing agents offer services for different destinations (Burundi, Rwanda), but some have a strong presence in a specific market.

For domestic traffic, market shares are fragmented, and the highest market share observed for a single clearing agent is 3.5 percent. The top 20 clearing agents only handle 35 percent of total domestic imports. In addition, these clearing agents do not have a strong presence in the transit market and focus mainly on domestic clearance operations because of the high perceived risk related to transit flows.

If we look at the characteristics of local imports and imports to landlocked countries, a standard operation consists of the clearance of a single 20-foot container for domestic imports and a single 40-foot container for transit traffic. The average number of containers per bill of lading is 1.83 for domestic traffic and 1.45 for transiting goods. About 90 percent of all bills of lading relate to one container. In a few cases, several containers are grouped in the same bill of lading, but this is rare. The maximum number of containers handled in the same bill of lading is 50 for domestic imports and 40 for transit imports, which translates into very few economies of scale for C&F and customs agents in general.

Average tonnage per container is higher for transit traffic than for local traffic (table 3.4). This is justified by the wider use of 40-foot containers for transit operations.

A main indicator of the efficiency of logistics operations in a port is average clearance time. However, the clearance process is a succession of operations, each leading to a specific delay. Using the customs release database, we consider individual data on two complementary operations that contribute to the overall delay in clearance: the payment of port dues and the physical transfer of containers to the client.

We can therefore monitor two aggregate delays: (a) time between unloading and payment of the invoice and (b) time between unloading and delivery to the client. The former is generally the main component of the latter, because cargo is retained within the port facilities until all taxes and dues have been paid. However, for a significant proportion of the sample, containers remain in the port despite the effective payment of all invoices.

Let us first focus on the aggregate delay between unloading of the container and final delivery to the client. Table 3.5 sums up the main statistics of this indicator across our sample. We consider the number of observations to be statistically significant enough to make general conclusions about the efficiency of port clearance operations.

Mean values are comparable for most destinations, with an average total delay of nine days for local imports and 12 days for transiting goods. Maximum and minimum values are also comparable for different destinations, with a 0-day minimum for a marginal set of urgent shipments well prepared in advance (1.38 percent for transit and 2.35 percent for local).

Table 3.4   Average Tonnage per Container for Local and Transit Containerized Imports in Dar es Salaam Port

Type of traffic	Tons	Number of containers	Average tons per hectare
Total	421,060	14,946	28
Local	302,840	11,116	27
Transit	118,220	3,830	31

Source: Dar es Salaam Port data for 2008.

Table 3.5   Statistical Distribution of Aggregate Delay between Unloading from Vessel and Final Delivery to the Client in Dar es Salaam Port, September to November 2008

Indicator	Local	All transit	Congo, Dem. Rep.	Zambia	Rwanda	Burundi	Uganda
Maximum	107	119	113	112	70	80	56
Minimum	0	0	0	0	0	0	0 .
Mean	13	15	15	16	11	16	11
Median	9	12	13	13	7	15	7
Standard deviations	13	13	12	13	11	12	12
Total traffic	302,840	118,180	50,060	27,600	21,000	14,880	2,760

Source: Dar es Salaam Port data for 2008.

Both types of traffic have long tails that reach 50 days for local imports and roughly 40 days for transit. A significant share of both types of traffic is handled in less than 10 days (46 percent for transit and 57 percent for local), which would be considered satisfactory by international standards.

This leads us to the assumption that average clearance delays are long because of a marginal proportion of problematic shipments. We can test this assumption by looking at the quartile distribution of each set of delays.

As shown in table 3.6, the middle 50 percent of the shipments for each destination is concentrated in the lower values of total clearance time (less than 30 percent of the maximum delay). This means that only a quarter of the shipments for each destination have a delivery time that considerably exceeds the mean value. It is therefore of the utmost importance to work on the quarter of shipments that are problematic, create congestion, and impede the other three-quarters of shipments.

As for cross-country comparison, longer dwell times are evident for Burundi, the Democratic Republic of Congo, and Zambia among transit countries, with typical dwell times of 13 to 25 days. Rwanda and Uganda have shorter average dwell times (11 days) for domestic traffic (13 days), which means that the clearance process is more efficient for these two countries. Median value is also inferior (seven compared with nine days). As for dispersion across the sample, the statistic for domestic traffic is very scattered, with a median value more than 10 times lower than the maximum value. This is also applicable for traffic in transit.

Table 3.6   Statistical Distribution of Dwell Time in Destination Countries, 2008

Indicator	Local	Transit	Burundi	Congo, Dem. Rep.	Rwanda	Uganda	Zambia
Minimum	0	0	0	0	0	0	0
First quartile	4	5	6	6	3	3	6
Median	9	12	15	13	7	7	13
Mean	13	15	16	15	11	11	16
Third quartile	17	22	24	21	15	16	23
Maximum	107	119	80	113	79	56	112

Source: Dar es Salaam Port data for 2008.

Median values are always inferior to mean values, as shown by the long tails leading to higher dwell times.

Irrespective of the destination country, dwell time of between five and 20 days is the most typical in Dar es Salaam port.

In conclusion, the situation in Dar es Salaam is not as bad as perceived (in the context of Sub-Saharan Africa). Approximately one-quarter of shipments are problematic, but mean dwell time is around one to two weeks. This is not up to the standards of the developed world, but it is rather good for a port in a Sub-Saharan African country.

In terms of benchmarking, since problematic shipments are difficult to eradicate, are related to governance or competency issues, and bias the mean dwell time, improving the performance of the first quartile or median should be the target. For Dar es Salaam, the goal should be set at between four and nine days for local traffic and at between five and 12 days for transit traffic.

Douala

Recent statistics from the container terminal operator indicate an average dwell time of 19.3 days for the first semester of 2010. This value has been quite stable in the last few years, despite strong and consistent growth in traffic (figure 3.6).[8]

Dwell time varies significantly, with a standard deviation equal to 160 percent of the mean value (table 3.7). A sequential analysis of delays shows that this variance is mainly the consequence of variance between vessel arrival and customs declaration lodging (referred to as "arrival to lodging" delays). Delay between payment of customs dues and gate exit ("payment to gate") also varies significantly according to shipment. These two intermediary delays account, on average, for 75 percent of total dwell time ("arrival to gate"). In contrast, the delay

Figure 3.6   Dwell Time in Douala Port, 2009

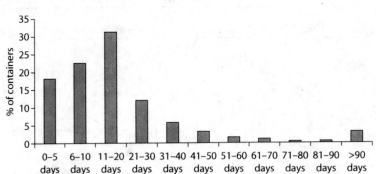

Source: Cameroonian customs data.
Note: Time between vessel discharge and gate exit.

Table 3.7   Statistical Distribution of Cargo Dwell Time in Douala Port, by Component, 2009

number of days

Indicator	Arrival to gate	Arrival to lodging	Lodging to payment	Payment to gate
Minimum	1	1	1	1
First quartile	8	3	1	1
Median	14	7	3	4
Mean	24.0	13.0	4.7	11.4
Third quartile	26	15	5	8
Maximum	566	446	340	387
Interquartile range	18	12	4	7

Source: Refas and Cantens 2011.

between lodging and payment of customs dues ("lodging to payment") is quite low.

For shippers (importers or exporters), dwell time in ports can include a temporary storage period, which is justified either by the time necessary to complete cargo clearance formalities (transactional dwell time) or by a decision to leave cargo in the port for a defined number of days after clearance (storage). Field investigations revealed that the latter case is common and that inventory management strategies coupled with negotiations of demurrage costs with shipping carriers cause shippers to use the port as a relatively cheap long-term warehouse. The desired cargo dwell time for most shippers ranges from five to 30 days for imports.[9]

Customs administration is also concerned with container dwell time because tax avoidance and cargo abandonment are associated with long dwell times.[10] In the port of Douala, there is a large dispersion of values in the distribution of dwell times, with a broad-tail shape that is quite specific to developing regions (figure 3.7).

The shape of the distribution, with a higher concentration of observations in lower values, demonstrates that all containers are not affected by long dwell time in the same way. A minority of containers (less than 25 percent) are affected by very long dwell times, while half of containers have acceptable values that range between 0 and 14 days. The 10-day gap between median and mean values is quite substantial and shows that policies targeting problematic segments (very long and abnormal delays) should be given high priority. The highest 15 values reported exceed 130 days, and some containers are yet to be cleared from port after a stay of more than 200 days.

An interesting feature of the distribution of cargo dwell times in Douala (verified over a two-year period) is the multimodality of the distribution (successive peaks). Possible explanations for the peaks observed include a psychological threshold linked to expiration of the free time period (an interesting opportunity to obtain free storage that shippers want to take full advantage of), expiration of negotiated free time (demurrage costs are most dissuasive in the first weeks), or negotiated objectives and application of penalties with brokers and agents (for example, clearance in less than two weeks or less than a month). Some seasonality is evident in these trends, with a more significant peak around 11 days in the second trimester of the year and a dominance of short

Figure 3.7   Cargo Dwell Time in Douala Port, 2009

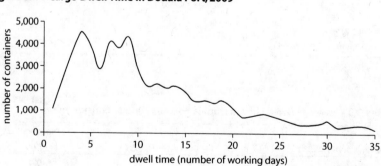

Source: Refas and Cantens 2011.

dwell times in the last trimester, but the general observance of discrete behaviors is consistent throughout the year.

In addition to these behavioral factors, shipment-level analysis also demonstrates that average dwell time varies across the sample according to cargo characteristics such as fiscal regime, bulking, density of value, and type of cargo.

Fiscal pressure seems to play a role in cargo dwell time. The correlation tends to be positive: higher fiscal pressure leads to higher dwell time, with a noticeable exception for duty-free items that have a relatively long average dwell time, despite the absence of duties; this could be linked to "bargaining time" between the customs broker and customs agent, a misclassification, a duty-free line, or simply the time to produce additional documents (table 3.8).

Bulking of containers also seems to play a role in the pattern of cargo dwell time: less-than-full-load containers take about three more days than full-load containers to be cleared from the port (table 3.9). This is paradoxical in the sense that bulking is usually performed by logistics providers with storage facilities outside the port, who should, in theory, want to minimize cargo stay in the port to maximize cargo stay in their own facilities. This could also be related to the fact that the risk of being inspected by customs may be higher if consolidated loads are not homogeneous.

Table 3.8   Average Dwell Time in Douala Port, by Range of Tariff Duties

Range of tariff duties	Average dwell time (days)	Number of containers
0% (duty free)	21.6	5,101
0–27.8% (necessity goods or duty free)	18.9	3,613
27.8–33.7% (raw materials)	19.2	6,676
33.7–45.7% (semifinished goods)	21.3	11,992
More than 46.7% (finished goods)	22.1	19,119

Source: Refas and Cantens 2011.

Table 3.9   Average Dwell Time in Douala Port, by Type of Consignment

Consignment type	Number of containers	Average dwell time (days)
Full container load	29,698	19.8
Less-than-full container load	26,524	22.6

Source: Refas and Cantens 2011.

Table 3.10   Average Dwell Time in Douala Port, by Density of Value

Density of value (FCFA per kilogram)	Number of containers	Average dwell time (days)	Arrival to lodging	Lodging to payment	Payment to gate
Less than 1,000	38,432	20.3	10.4	4.3	5.9
1,000–6,500	15,092	22.8	12.1	4.4	6.6
More than 6,500	2,318	24.7	12.4	4.9	7.5

Source: Refas and Cantens 2011.
Note: FCFA = Franc Communauté Financière Africaine.

Density of value is an important determinant of logistics strategies, as it is a leading driver of holding and transportation costs (table 3.10). An analysis of cargo dwell times and density of value confirms the crucial importance of this variable. The correlation is positive: higher cargo value leads to higher dwell times. The analysis of gaps between the three categories leads to the conclusion that low-value goods exit the port faster than high-value goods (about two days faster on average), which would reflect a better performance of both shippers and brokers.

This may seem counterintuitive because owners of high-value cargo should exert more pressure to move their goods out of the port quickly. However, tariff duties are higher for high-value goods, and agents put them under more scrutiny than low-value goods in an effort to limit fraud. This would explain why high-value goods have longer dwell times.

The variety of imports is significant at the country level, and a thorough analysis of cargo dwell time by commodity is difficult. Looking at different categories of cargo, however, using the two-digit Harmonized System code provides a broad sense of the patterns of clearance by type of cargo. We use 15 categories, most of which account for at least 5 percent of the total volume of imports. Table 3.11 shows the significant variance of average dwell time across different categories. While chemicals and allied industries are cleared in 16 days, on average, finished goods, such as machinery, foodstuffs, or transport vehicles and parts, remain in the port terminal for more than 24 days, on average. Further understanding of these differences is needed, and it is important to look at inventory management strategies in particular. In the meantime, this brief analysis confirms that the type of commodity is a crucial determinant of cargo dwell time.

Finally, the operations of third parties such as C&F agents, shipping agents, or shipping lines play an important role in cargo dwell time and

Table 3.11   Average Dwell Time in Douala Port, by Type of Commodity

Product category	Average dwell time (days)	Number of containers	% of containers
Chemicals and allied industries	16.4	5,945	13
Foodstuffs	24.2	5,744	12
Plastics and rubber	21.5	4,883	11'
Machinery electrical	24.3	4,773	10
Stone and glass	22.9	4,036	9
Metals	19.9	3,589	8
Textiles	19.9	3,571	8
Vegetable products	21.4	3,430	7
Miscellaneous	23.1	2,646	6
Wood and wooden products	18.0	2,431	5
Mineral products	18.0	2,418	5
Transportation	26.2	1,623	3
Footwear and headgear	16.2	593	1
Raw hides, skins, leather, and furs	18.4	558	1
Other	30.9	261	1

Source: Refas and Cantens 2011.

so need to be examined. The specific context of the port of Douala is of importance when interpreting high dwell times.

The C&F market is very concentrated in Douala, with an aggregate market share of the 20 biggest agents that exceeds 55 percent for container imports destined for local consumption. Despite the increase in the number of C&F agents in operation (4 percent growth annually), the top players gain market share every year.

This concentration has two adverse effects on dwell times: first, the weak negotiating power of clients with the main C&F agents leads to a low level of service; second, low-cost, unprofessional C&F agents have no choice but to compete for the rest of the market on price at the expense of quality.

As shown in tables 3.12 and 3.13, the time efficiency of the major C&F agents for successive operations before the container exits the port is poor, in the lowest percentiles. The performance of C&F agents seems to be rather idiosyncratic. However, due to their existing market share and market concentration, their poor performance does not hamper their development (and they probably pass on to the consumer their internal deficiencies).

Efficient international trade logistics require standardization and predictability. However, this standardization can hardly be reached when shippers operate with a small number of containers per shipment and a

Table 3.12   C&F Market Concentration in Douala Port, 2007–10
% of declarations

Rank by market share	2007	2008	2009	2010
Top three C&F agents	18	17	18	20
Top seven C&F agents	31	30	31	33
Top 20 C&F agents	57	51	56	56
Total number of agents	145	151	156	162

Source: Refas and Cantens 2011.

Table 3.13   Time Performance of Main Customs Brokers in Douala Port
relative performance (percentile)

Rank of C&F agent	Time between arrival and lodging	Time between lodging and liquidation	Time between liquidation and payment	Time between payment and gate exit
1	8	87	58	95
2	50	58	60	76
3	25	74	41	78
4	51	28	64	41
5	59	19	61	52
6	17	9	83	90
7	50	54	75	50
8	62	20	82	23
9	48	56	94	61
10	74	50	81	34

Source: Refas and Cantens 2011.
Note: Percentile means the rank of the C&F agent for the various steps among all the C&F agents.

low volume of shipments per year. The average number of containers per bill of lading in the port of Douala was 2.2 in 2009. Few shippers have regular shipments, and the vast majority of flow is ordered by medium or small companies that import fewer than five containers a year. The feedback from major C&F agents and port players is that these companies do not import regularly enough to have standard and robust processes in place. They have little control over import logistics, and they often fail to forecast delays in the logistics chain consistently. This is why they face much inefficiency in the clearance process, including errors in customs declarations, delays in transmission of import documents by suppliers, or shortages of liquidity, and this inefficiency is synonymous with long delays and high costs. The impact of unpredictability on logistics costs is an estimated 25–30 percent of the factory price (Arvis, Raballand, and Marteau 2010), while the impact on delays is in days.

Another significant pattern for container imports passing through the port of Douala is the concentration of shipping flows along a few main shipping routes. The top three shipping routes account for 70 percent of total imports (table 3.14). This disrupts the pattern of arrivals and creates congestion in the clearance process (transfer to the yard, customs clearance formalities) that generates delays throughout the chain of operations.

Finally, the pattern of maritime transport operations may be one of the main determinants of inefficient cargo clearance. Two transshipment hubs (Algeciras and Las Palmas) account for more than 55 percent of the total volume of imports, and the top six origins are all transshipment hubs that together account for 87 percent of total volume. The top two routes (Algeciras-Douala and Las Palmas–Douala) are also the only two routes that run with a fixed day of arrival (Friday and Saturday, respectively). As a consequence, Fridays and Saturdays are the busiest days of the week and account for more than half of total traffic (table 3.15). This affects the performance of clearance operations and encourages shippers to deal

Table 3.14   Concentration of Container Imports along Main Shipping Routes for Douala Port

Port of origin	% of container imports	Cumulative %
Algéciras	34	34
Las Palmas	22	56
Antwerp	14	70
Singapore	11	81
Dubai	3	84
Genoa	3	87

Source: Refas and Cantens 2011.

Table 3.15   Daily Distribution of Clearance Operations in Douala
% of operations

Day	Container discharge	Declaration lodging	Payment of dues	Issuance of exit bill	Exit from yard
Monday	8	25	17	15	15
Tuesday	7	20	23	20	18
Wednesday	7	18	20	21	20
Thursday	9	19	20	21	19
Friday	39	18	19	20	21
Saturday	16	0	0	4	6
Sunday	15	0	0	0	0

Source: Refas and Cantens 2011.

with clearance operations on a weekly schedule, as was confirmed in local interviews.

Another symptom of this lack of awareness of total logistics costs is the indifference to variability of arrival day. Maersk Line is the only shipping line that has implemented a fixed weekly schedule on its main route, which, in theory, should help shippers to improve the quality of forecasts and reduce inventory levels. Mediterranean Shipping Company also has recently implemented a fixed schedule for one of its main connections. For all other regular calls, the arrival day is variable, which introduces uncertainty and variability in operational schedules, to the benefit of the shipping line but to the detriment of shippers and the terminal operating company.

This chapter, based on shipment-level analysis, has demonstrated that the characteristics of demand matter a lot for the distribution of cargo dwell time. Therefore, firm surveys were undertaken in five countries in Sub-Saharan Africa to assess the main determinants of demand for short or long cargo dwell time. The results are presented in chapter 4.

Notes

1. For more detailed information on the case studies, see appendix A.
2. Storage delay is not isolated, because a slow consignee will also act slowly regarding the transaction. For the sake of simplicity, all of the "voluntary" delays are put under storage.
3. Transshipments account for approximately 20 percent of total cargo.
4. Free time is defined as the time from when the vessel completes discharge and the container is stored in the port area without incurring any port storage charges. This is set at three days for import containers and seven days for transit containers.
5. For transit cargo, the average dwell time would be one or two days more because of the need to secure a bond, unload the cargo, and arrange for the inland bonded movement. For outbound containers, both loaded and empty boxes are delivered to the container terminal about three days prior to the vessel's arrival.
6. Once declared as unclaimed, customs publishes a list of these containers. This usually requires about a month. Next, the contents of the containers are catalogued and a reserve price is set before the auction takes place. Altogether, the process requires at least 60 days. It is especially difficult for consolidated

shipments with a large amount of goods, especially used clothing. This procedure cannot be applied to government cargo.

7. The container terminal in Dar es Salaam was concessioned in 2000.

8. Container traffic represents about 45 percent of the total tonnage that transits through the port of Douala annually. Containers are also the primary mode of transport for Cameroonian exports, representing about 75 percent of total traffic in tons and about 45 percent of Cameroonian imports.

9. Free time at the terminal—the period during which a container can reside in the container yard without being assessed a demurrage fee—has been set at 11 days since the concession contract was signed in 2005; this is a somewhat long free time given the level of congestion in the port.

10. Article 108 of the customs code of the Central African Economic and Monetary Community defines a maximum clearance delay beyond which cargo is confiscated and put under bonded storage. This delay is currently 90 days in Douala, after which the cargo is auctioned.

References

Arvis, Jean-François, Gaël Raballand, and Jean-François Marteau. 2010. *The Cost of Being Landlocked: Logistic Costs and Supply Chain Reliability.* Washington, DC: World Bank.

Djeuwo, Marcellin. 2011. "The Cameroonian Experience of Reform and Its Impact on Clearance and Dwell Time." Presentation at the Tunis stakeholder workshop, December 13.

Farrell, Sheila. 2009. "Factors Influencing Port Efficiency: A Case Study of Dar es Salaam." Paper presented at a conference of the International Association of Maritime Economics, Copenhagen, June 24–26.

Refas, Salim, and Thomas Cantens. 2011. "Why Does Cargo Spend Weeks in African Ports? The Case of Douala, Cameroon." Policy Research Working Paper 5565, World Bank, Washington, DC.

CHAPTER 4

The Impact of Demand on Container Dwell Time

The case studies and shipment-level analysis of dwell time presented in chapter 3 show that long dwell times (which account for a large share of containers in terminals) are one of the key issues that need to be addressed (probably across the continent) and are related mostly to factors under the control of shippers. This confirms one of the initial hypotheses of this work, which is that the behaviors and strategies of shippers have an impact on dwell time in ports. The demand by importers for port dwell time beyond the time required to complete port operations and transactions seems to be related mainly to inventory management and the "business model" used (including the extent of informal practices).

Due to the fact that demand from importers seems to explain a large part of long-dwell cargo, in this chapter we present theoretical foundations explaining current demand in Sub-Saharan Africa and then present some statistical analysis, based mainly on firm surveys.[1]

Some Theoretical Considerations

The model examines cost minimization strategies and profit maximization strategies. Coupled with various market structures, it seeks to explain why behaviors that are perceived as irrational, such as leaving cargo in the port, are the best option for an importer.

Cost Minimization Strategies

The application of the cost minimization model presented in appendix B leads to the expected conclusion that, because additional dwell time results in additional logistics costs, any market player seeking to minimize its total logistics costs will try to reduce port dwell time. We also reach two secondary conclusions of importance.

The first pertains to the impact of dwell time on replenishment time. Our analysis shows that the optimized interval time between reorders is inversely proportionate to dwell time in the port. An inefficient port clearance system with very long clearance time would therefore encourage shippers to replenish their cargo at shorter intervals and to split their annual orders into smaller and more frequent batches for delivery.

The second pertains to the arbitrage between different warehousing options. Modern container shipping operations should facilitate the movement of goods along chains, and ports should be nothing more than gateways.

In the new paradigm of "warehousing-derived terminalization," port terminals tend to replace warehousing facilities and gradually become strategic storage units. Our analysis shows that companies seeking to minimize total logistics costs will leave their cargo in the port when the financial cost of clearing it outweighs the potential savings from not storing it in private or third-party facilities outside the port.

In this situation, there is no incentive to clear the cargo from the port storage area, even if storage costs are high (parking costs plus demurrage fees); the move to cheaper storage facilities outside the port will only occur after cargo has spent a long time stored in the port. Also shippers might be willing to leave their cargo in the container terminal or in off-dock container yards (ODCYs) if they cannot bear the financial cost of paying all port clearance charges and fees in advance. They will not move their cargo until they have sold it and are able to pay these expenses.

Profit Maximization Strategies

Analysis of total logistics costs provides useful insights into the reasons why shippers might seek to reduce port dwell times. However, cost minimization does not explain the variety of strategies observed with regard to port dwell time, including the paradoxical situation where shippers are indifferent to long or very long dwell times.

The analysis of free competition does not depart from the conclusions of the cost minimization analysis, but the analysis of monopolies does provide useful insights into profit maximization strategies. We show first that, despite being a cost setter, a rational monopolist should seek to reduce port dwell times to optimize profits because it is not possible to pass on all costs to the clients without losing sales. In a situation where demand is inelastic to price, modeled through the kinked curve theory, we show that the monopolist is not affected in the short term by higher logistics costs and therefore makes no effort to reduce dwell times. Such a scenario is likely to happen for patterns of cyclical demand that are elastic to price only in the long term (for example, food supplies, drugs, and equipment), while in the short term, there is little demand risk and the monopolist is therefore indifferent to higher logistics costs due to longer dwell times. A third pricing behavior derived from this situation of inelastic demand and observed among monopolistic companies is opportunistic pricing, which explains some paradoxical situations in which companies are willing to suffer from adverse logistics conditions because doing so helps them to justify charging higher markups or holding inventories longer in order to speculate on higher sale prices.

Companies seldom operate as pure monopolies, however, and the distribution of market power is more often in the hands of a few firms—that is, an oligopolistic situation. We analyze different cases of oligopolies in turn: cartels, leader-followers, price war (Bertrand competition), Nash equilibria–Cournot competition, and kinked oligopoly. All of these situations lead to different behaviors. In a cartel or leader-follower situation, monopolistic pricing strategies are observed. In a price war situation, the market behaves in the same way as in free competition, and companies try to minimize dwell time and logistics costs to secure competitive advantage over other market players. In other situations, the unpredictable consequences of price changes discourage the few market players from undertaking any price move that may unbalance the system; as a consequence, prices are stable despite changing logistics conditions.

Uncertainty

Taking uncertainty into account does not radically change the dynamics of cost minimization or profit maximization; in fact, it strengthens the conclusions in the previous chapters. We show that because of the risk of losing profit, companies operating in an uncertain context and lacking visibility on actual delivery times will behave with excess caution, accepting longer dwell times and building time for delay into their production or trading schedule to plan for the worst situation. This leads to longer dwell times in port, despite the adverse impact on costs and profits, because the long dwell time that is built into the business model, expenditures, and logistics, especially for landlocked countries, is not designed for fast clearance (and payment).

An Empirical Analysis of Demand: Lack of Competence or Purpose?

A key factor is the lack of competence and professionalism of small importers and customs brokers, who often do not exercise due diligence in the clearance process. This results in considerable delays in payment and slows down the entire logistics chain. The capacity and professionalism of the private sector have a large effect on the clearing process, even greater than expected. For instance, an analysis of Douala port by a major freight forwarder found that customs procedures cause only 1 percent of all abnormal—20 days or more—cargo delays. The same analysis calculated that lack of or erroneous documentation by the importer or delays by the pre-inspection company are far more time-consuming than customs procedures in total clearance time.

Empirical Evidence in the Ports of Douala (Cameroon) and Lomé (Togo)

Douala

In Douala, the high level of inventory coverage leads to long port storage times. Using a typical private storage cost of FCFA 100 per ton per day,[2] we estimate that storage in the port of Douala is cheaper than outside storage for 22 days, meaning 11 days more than the container terminal's free time![3] As long as most shippers do not intend to reduce inventory levels sharply, cargo dwell times will remain very high in the port of Douala.

The situation could improve slightly if shippers were aware of the total logistics costs associated with long cargo dwell times. Few operators include hedging costs or financial charges in their calculation of factory prices, and even fewer envisage actions to reduce dwell times with the objective of reducing inventory levels. As a consequence, dwell time in ports appears simply as an alternative to dwell time in private facilities, and shippers do not undertake a comprehensive analysis of lead time and inventory levels. Shippers who have high inventory coverage (typically two or three months) do not experience a major direct impact on costs because long dwell times are simply an alternative to costly and physically limited private storage.

However, the situation is radically different for shippers that have low inventory coverage, have just-in-time production processes, or handle urgent shipments. In these cases, the direct costs of higher cargo dwell time in port are not offset by savings in private storage costs since cargo is used or sold as soon as it arrives in the shipper's facilities. In other words, storage in port is not perceived as an alternative to storage in private facilities but rather as a pure delay in the supply chain that affects logistics costs and customer service. The direct costs of long dwell times would quickly become prohibitive, especially in terms of lost sales (an estimated 0.5 percent a day).

The contracting patterns of clearing and forwarding (C&F) agents also exhibit some revealing peculiarities. For example, the introduction of a time-efficiency indicator with a weight of 30 percent in the national evaluation framework of C&F agents (Label Qualité des Commissionnaires Agréés en Douane) suggests that shippers are aware of the importance of time efficiency. However, few shippers include compelling time-efficiency terms into their contracts with C&F agents, especially dominant C&F agents who have a very strong supplier power. Those shippers who do include performance conditions in their C&F contracts formulate them in a way that leaves room for argument (for example, maximum clearance time on the condition that all documents are submitted correctly and in a timely manner by shippers). This is why the largest brokers maintain very high market shares despite poor time performance. Another key factor is that subsidiaries of international trade and industrial firms are often either financially linked with international forwarders or contractually linked to them at the regional or continental level, which does not encourage efficiency at the country level.

There are good reasons to believe that wider recognition of the national broker's label would slowly increase the number of requirements placed on customs brokers, but that shippers would have to replace brokers with whom they have contracted for years. This seems improbable due to very strong patterns of repeat buying (loyalty of shippers).

Another major issue is the availability of cash and the strategies of shippers to reduce their financial exposure. Because of costly trade borrowing and limited import financing tools, shippers are often short of cash in their daily operations, and this is a major hindrance to the reduction of dwell times. The bulk of customs declaration lodging is done in the second or third week after container discharge, even though it takes no longer than three days, on average, to clear customs.

In the first step (the processing of payments), which takes 13 days on average today, processing could be shortened by facilitating the financing of customs dues, because finding the money to pay customs dues is a major reason for delaying this step. Savings in opportunity costs and financial charges associated with delayed clearance are probably underestimated because severe cash constraints and very high opportunity costs sometimes offset high demurrage charges after an extended stay in the terminal.

Some shippers facing extreme cash constraints have no choice but to abandon cargo in the port because they are unable to pay customs dues and clearance charges or can only pay them after part of the shipment has been sold.

Lomé

In Togo, the local market for consumer goods and food products is dominated by a few medium-size companies and strong informal operators who have captured significant market share over years in the context of a fragile administration and macroeconomic difficulties. Established companies use their own storage facilities in the city of Lomé adjacent to the port. All other operators take advantage of low storage prices to leave cargo in the port until final sale. Port warehousing areas have large capacity that has not yet been fully exploited, and this has delayed the development of off-dock storage. In addition, the trucking and freight-forwarding markets are scattered among a large number of small operators, especially in the important transit markets.

Storage practices are difficult to track in Lomé in the absence of comprehensive customs data. However, comprehensive port delay statistics suggest that delay is due in large part to the behavior of shippers (figure 4.1). For example, there are significant peaks in dwell time frequencies at two weeks, three weeks, and four weeks, although clearance formalities take only about seven days. The port authority in Lomé seems unable to track the payment of parking fees or to identify storage practices.

Findings from the Firm Surveys

The main objective of the analysis of firm surveys is to identify shippers' demand and practices related to perceived and actual cargo dwell time and how they are linked to private sector market structure.

Figure 4.1   Container Dwell Time in Lomé Port, 2009

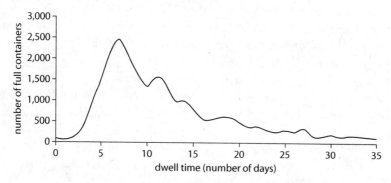

Source: Authors based on data from Autonomous Port of Lomé.

The statistical analysis of the results of firm surveys attempts to validate some of the theoretical assumptions presented in the previous section. The surveys were conducted in five Sub-Saharan African countries—Kenya, Nigeria, South Africa, Uganda, and Zambia—from May to July 2011. Each of the surveys includes about 100 observations (per country), yielding 506 validated records. Participants in the survey are shippers importing containerized cargo through the ports of Durban (for South African and Zambian importers),[4] Mombasa (for Kenyan and Ugandan importers), and Lagos (for Nigerian importers). Both manufacturers and retailers in the most important sectors are represented in the survey.[5]

Data Collection Problems Encountered during Fieldwork

Several problems were encountered while collecting data in the field. In many instances, the respondents were not able to answer all of the questions, mostly because they did not have the information (they had to check with other employees or the forwarding agents). For example, many respondents did not know clearance times in harbor or customs, as clearance procedures are generally handled by their C&F agents, who do not necessarily share the information with them. Many shippers were only concerned with the final on-site delivery dates. Some respondents did not understand the questions, even though pilot surveys had been conducted to eliminate this problem.[6] These issues reveal the problem of information asymmetry between importers and their C&F agents, owing mainly to the lack professionalism and transparency of C&F agents, who do not provide feedback about their work or exchange information about the clearance process with their shippers.

Another issue, particularly in Kenya, Nigeria, and Uganda, is that some of the potential respondents were suspicious about the survey and not willing to participate in studies of this nature. They considered the questionnaire to be seeking sensitive or private information.

However, several respondents, mostly in South Africa, felt that the interview was interesting and expressed appreciation that it was being conducted because they felt that something needed to be done to "improve the red tape of getting goods out of the harbor in time."

This demonstrates two major problems that inhibit change: lack of information and low expectations.

Dwell Time Statistics and Expectations

The perception about what is "normal" cargo dwell time varies between countries and regions. Refas and Cantens (2011) present a detailed discussion regarding what is considered "normal" dwell time in Sub-Saharan Africa. According to them, it is around 11 days (close to the free time period) in Douala and in most ports in Sub-Saharan Africa. This is a particularity of the region, because the dwell time perceived as "normal" in most international ports in East Asia or Europe is around four days.

Dwell Time as reported by shippers. In the surveys, two variables were used to measure cargo dwell time: (a) the average dwell time measured in days and (b) the distribution of dwell time, by length of time: 0–5 days, 6–10 days, 11–20 days, 21–40 days, 41–70 days, and more than 70 days.[7] The average cargo dwell time (measured in days) by country, weighted by the number of imported containers, is shown in figure 4.2. South Africa has the shortest dwell time, as expected, close to what is identified as "normal" in Europe or Asia. Nigeria has the longest. The average dwell time of the total five countries sample is around 8 days.

These figures should be viewed with caution, because they are not necessarily representative and are less reliable than customs data. Data collected in firm surveys should only be used as a complement to customs data on dwell time.

It is also interesting to analyze the distribution of dwell time by country (figure 4.3). In South Africa, 93 percent of imported containers have a dwell time between 0 and 5 days, which is expected, since the average is very low (3.93 days) compared to the other countries. In Kenya and Nigeria, 69 and 74 percent, respectively, of their imports need between

Figure 4.2   Cargo Dwell Times in Select African Countries, Weighted by the Number of Imported Containers, 2011

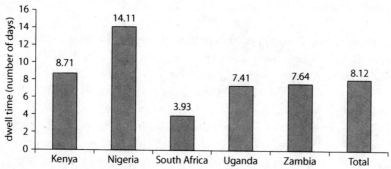

Source: Authors based on firm surveys.

Figure 4.3   Cargo Dwell Times in Select African Countries, by the Percentage of Containers, 2011

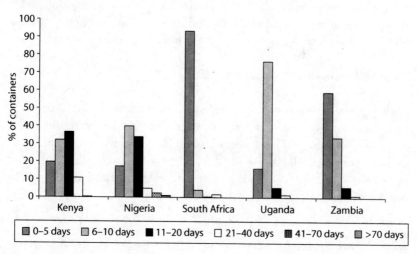

Source: Authors based on firm surveys.

6 and 20 days to be cleared; this is consistent with the average dwell time experienced by Kenya (around nine) and Nigeria (around 14 days).

In Zambia, most of the imported containers (59 percent) have a dwell time between 0 and 5 days; hence average dwell time is almost the same in Zambia (7.64 days) as in Uganda (7.41 days), even though only 16 percent of containers in Uganda have average dwell time of 0 to 5 days, while 76 percent have average dwell time of 6 to 11 days.

Zambian importers benefit from the relatively good performance of Durban port, which shows that tackling performance issues in a port has a positive spillover effect on landlocked countries.

Comparison with shippers' perception of dwell time. When importers' perceptions of cargo dwell time are compared with actual dwell time in Sub-Saharan African countries, the latter is higher than expected in Kenya and Nigeria, which means that importers here are likely to want to reduce dwell time and might exert pressure to do so.

On the contrary, in South Africa, Uganda, and Zambia, the perception of normal cargo dwell time is higher than the estimated normal dwell time, meaning that there may not be strong pressure to lower it; importers might be satisfied with experiencing a shorter dwell time than expected. In both cases, average dwell time is lower in Durban than in the other ports studied, which may explain the relatively low expectations.

These differences between countries suggest that dwell time is also about perception and information (table 4.1). Shippers may not understand the significance of dwell time and may not have accurate information on it (dwell time statistics are often unknown and incorrect).

Analysis by Importers' Characteristics

Main activity. The analysis of average dwell time with regard to the shippers' main activity indicates that manufacturers perform better than traders overall (figure 4.4). Moreover, manufacturers have a significantly shorter average dwell time—one day shorter—than the other importers ($t(313.826) = 1.679; p = 0.047$).[8] They are more efficient and should be the primary counterparts of customs or terminals in contractualization

Table 4.1   Average Dwell Time and the Perception of Normal Dwell Time in Select African Countries, 2011

dwell time (number of days)

Indicator	Kenya	Nigeria	South Africa	Uganda	Zambia
Port	Mombasa	Lagos	Durban	Mombasa	Durban
Actual average cargo dwell time	8.71	14.11	3.93	7.41	7.64
Perception of "normal" average cargo dwell time	7.7	11.2	6.5	8.7	14.1

Source: Authors based on firm surveys.

Figure 4.4   Cargo Dwell Time, by Shippers' Main Activity, 2011

Source: Authors based on firm surveys.

initiatives because they master their logistics (raw materials or intermediary products) and can reach top performance by implementing efficient processes.

Furthermore, small and medium retailers experience the longest dwell time. They have a significantly longer dwell time than the other shippers—around 10 days longer ($t(9.056) = 1.7991$; $p = 0.05$). This is not surprising: small retailers generally do not have their own warehouse and probably use the port as a storage facility; they may also experience a slower clearance process than larger shippers. This may be due to informal practices and possible "negotiations" with regard to lowering tariff duties and thus the cost of imports.

These findings are consistent with the assumption of the theoretical model, which posits that companies intentionally leave their cargo in ports since these are cheap storage units. The analysis by country illustrates that small and medium retailers are more likely to experience long dwell times in Nigeria, Zambia, Uganda, and, to a lesser extent, South Africa, which confirms our assumptions (figure 4.5).

The preponderance of trading is self-reinforcing: retailers have longer dwell times, and this makes port dwell time longer for everyone. This constitutes a barrier to assembling industries, which then paves the way for retailers to constitute a large share of port users.

Volume of importations. Contrary to the common belief that the volume of imports is an important determinant of cargo dwell time, in

Figure 4.5   Cargo Dwell Times in Select African Countries, by Shippers' Main Activity, 2011

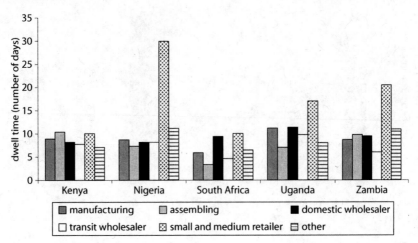

Source: Authors based on firm surveys.

Sub-Saharan Africa the volume of imports is not correlated with dwell time (figure 4.6). Hence, shippers that import medium volumes seem to have significantly longer dwell time—about one day longer—compared to shippers that import very low, low, and large volumes $(t(212.253) = 1.669; p = 0.048)$. And shippers importing large volumes seem to have significantly shorter dwell time—approximately one day shorter—than all the other shippers $(t(268.041) = 2.218; p = 0.013)$. More than the size of the company, the type of company and its business model are what matter the most.

Frequency of deliveries. An important relationship to test through data analysis is the one between dwell time and the annual frequency of deliveries. It seems that more frequent deliveries—more than 10 deliveries every year (figure 4.7)—result in about two days shorter dwell time $(t(273.202)= 3.562; p = 0.0002)$. This reflects the dominant situation of importers in Sub-Saharan African countries, who have, on average, less than 10 deliveries every year and do not have real logistics strategies in place.

Analysis by Market Structure

Figures 4.8 and 4.9 present dwell time by the level of competition between shippers. In figure 4.8, the categories 0, 1, and 2–5 competitors are aggregated into "monopoly-oligopoly," and the categories 6–20 and

Figure 4.6   Cargo Dwell Time, by Annual Volume of Imports, 2011

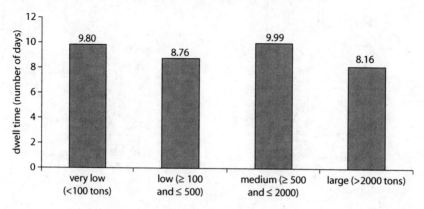

Source: Authors based on firm surveys.

Figure 4.7   Cargo Dwell Time, by Annual Frequency of Deliveries, 2011

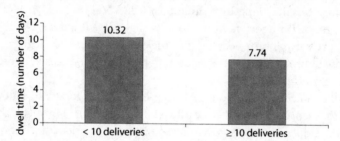

Source: Authors based on firm surveys.

Figure 4.8   Cargo Dwell Time, by Number of Competitors, 2011

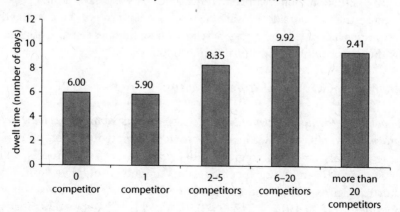

Source: Authors based on firm surveys.

Figure 4.9   Cargo Dwell Time, Monopoly-Oligopoly versus Competition, 2011

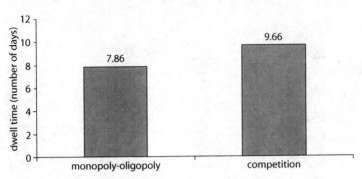

Source: Authors based on firm surveys.

more than 20 competitors are aggregated into "competition." Importers in monopoly-oligopoly situations experience a two-day shorter dwell time than importers in competitive situations ($t(223.564) = 2.694; p = 0.003$).[9] In fact, rational importers in monopoly-oligopoly situations are likely to have shorter dwell time because they seek to minimize their logistics costs (long dwell time generally translates into higher logistics costs) in order to optimize their profits.

In all countries except South Africa, monopoly-oligopoly situations are likely to keep cargo dwell times lower (figure 4.10). However, shorter dwell time does not necessarily translate into lower prices, since the main objective of shippers is to maximize profits.

Only in South Africa does the high degree of competition play an important part in keeping dwell time shorter: since importers in a competitive situation cannot afford to reflect the costs of delays in their prices because they are afraid of losing customers, they protect the customers from price increases due to cost increases. These findings can be explained by the maturity of the South African economy.

Analysis by C&F Agents' Professionalism

Level of information provided by C&F agents about the clearance process. Overall, when C&F agents provide accurate forecasts and real-time information about progress or delay in the clearance process well in advance (even if unexpected events might arise), dwell time is shorter (figure 4.11)—one day shorter when real-time information is provided ($t(184.615) = 2.242; p = 0.013$) and less than one day shorter

Figure 4.10   Cargo Dwell Times in Select African Countries, Monopoly-Oligopoly versus Competition, 2011

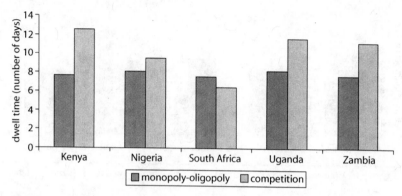

Source: Authors based on firm surveys.

Figure 4.11   Cargo Dwell Time, by Level of Information about the Clearance Process Provided by C&F Agents, 2011

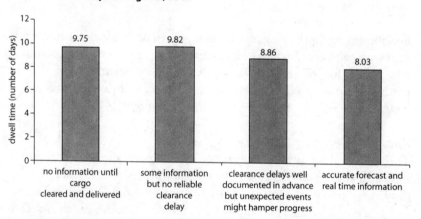

Source: Authors based on firm surveys.

when clearance delays are well documented in advance, although this is not significant ($t(157.338) = 0.535$; $p = 0.296$). Shippers who master their logistics are the most efficient. The information appears to be the key to improve performance.

These findings hold for Kenya, South Africa, and, to a lesser extent, Uganda (figure 4.12).

Main determinants in the selection of C&F agents. When shippers select C&F agents based on their professionalism, cargo dwell time is likely to

Figure 4.12   Cargo Dwell Times in Select African Countries, by the Level of Information about the Clearance Process Provided by C&F Agents, 2011

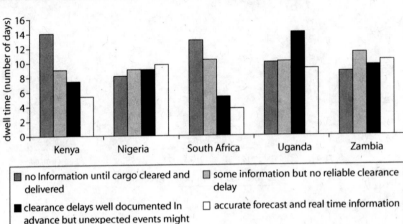

Source: Authors based on firm surveys.

be shorter than in the case of a selection based on the long term relationship with the agent (figure 4.13). Hence, when costs are the most important reason for selecting an agent, dwell time is shorter. However, the picture is not clear when looking at the data by country and may reflect a misunderstanding of the questions asked (figure 4.14).

Analysis by Product Category

The overall distribution of imports by category, shown in table 4.2, indicates that machinery and electrical products are the largest category (27 percent), followed by chemicals and allied industries (14 percent) and transportation (13 percent).[10] Machinery and electrical is the largest category in Nigeria, South Africa, and Uganda and the smallest in Zambia. While the distribution of most product categories is rather balanced among countries, important differences are evident for transportation, which accounts for 30 percent of imports in Zambia, but only 5 percent in South Africa. The differences are also important for textiles, which account for only 0–4 percent of imports in all countries, except South Africa (16 percent).

This might explain a certain selection bias in favor of equipment, but also a higher level of professionalism (in South Africa compared to the other four countries) and therefore might depict the situation as better

Figure 4.13   Cargo Dwell Time, by the Main Factors in Selecting C&F Agents, 2011

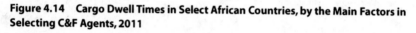

Source: Authors based on firm surveys.

Figure 4.14   Cargo Dwell Times in Select African Countries, by the Main Factors in Selecting C&F Agents, 2011

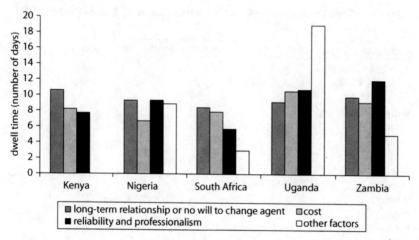

Source: Authors based on firm surveys.

than it is in reality. Moreover, the category of service products is small overall (2 percent) and nonexistent in Nigeria and Zambia.

Average dwell time varies significantly across categories and countries (table 4.3). For example, stone and glass products remain in port terminals for about 12 days. They are cleared more rapidly in South Africa

Table 4.2   Imports in Select African Countries, by Product Category, 2011
% of all imports

Product category	Total	Kenya	Nigeria	South Africa	Uganda	Zambia
Chemicals and allied industries	14	18	15	11	12	11
Foodstuffs	9	10	15	5	7	7
Machinery and electrical	27	25	32	30	30	18
Mineral products and metals	9	12	17	9	4	5
Miscellaneous	4	4	0	9	5	4
Plastics and rubbers	6	6	3	9	7	2
Service	2	4	0	2	1	0
Stone and glass	7	2	7	4	10	16
Textiles	5	4	0	16	4	2
Transportation	13	6	10	5	15	30
Wood and wooden products	4	8	2	0	5	5

Source: Authors based on firm surveys.

Table 4.3   Cargo Dwell Times in Select African Countries, by Type of Product, 2011
number of days

Product category	Total	Kenya	Nigeria	South Africa	Uganda	Zambia
Chemicals and allied industries	9.94	10.44	9.33	8.83	8.90	12.33
Foodstuffs	7.65	5.89	7.67	5.00	9.33	11.00
Machinery and electrical	9.03	7.68	9.32	8.35	10.56	8.80
Mineral products and metals	7.94	7.18	8.10	5.40	7.00	15.33
Miscellaneous	11.93	12.25	—	11.80	10.75	14.00
Plastics and rubber	8.89	6.60	9.50	3.60	14.83	10.00
Service	7.17	6.50	—	14.00	3.00	—
Stone and glass	12.28	10.00	9.75	4.50	13.75	14.33
Textiles	6.53	6.50	—	5.11	10.00	9.00
Transportation	9.21	13.20	8.67	3.67	11.83	7.35
Wood and wooden products	8.27	8.29	7.00	—	7.25	10.00

Source: Authors based on firm surveys.
Note: — = Not available.

(4.5 days) than in Zambia (14 days), which may explain differences in the degree of competition in Zambia and South Africa.

Moreover, while textiles take 6.5 days to clear on average, they take only 5 days in South Africa and 10 days in Uganda. These findings confirm that the type of commodity is an important determinant of cargo dwell time.

Finally, table 4.4 summarizes the main assumptions of the theoretical model and the findings of the statistical analysis.

This exercise is, to our knowledge, the first of its type and does not answer all of the questions raised in this field. However, it demonstrates the crucial importance of studying private sector practices and incentives before designing any program aiming to reduce dwell time. The assumption that "importers are the victims of long container dwell time" is likely to be wrong in the case of many ports in Sub-Saharan Africa, which probably explains the multiple failures of many initiatives in this area. Only a couple of importers may be on the side of reform (for example, in Cameroon). This kind of study should be expanded to other countries, and some

Table 4.4   Theoretical Assumptions and Findings from the Statistical Analysis

Theoretical assumptions	Survey findings
Warehousing-derived terminalization: terminals are cheap storage units for shippers (for example, port storage is a cheaper option until 22 days in Douala).	Verified. Small and medium retailers are likely to use the port as a cheap storage facility.
Product characteristics and market structure are the main determinants of dwell time.	Verified for market structure. Monopolies are time-efficient in Kenya, Nigeria, Uganda, and Zambia, but competition is time-efficient in South Africa. Hence, low dwell time is not necessarily reflected in lower prices in the case of monopolies-oligopolies (which might seek to maximize profits); however, it might keep prices low in competitive situations (South Africa). Verified for product category. Important differences are found in cargo dwell time among product categories.
Dwell time is also about perception and information. In uncertain contexts, shippers build delay into their production schedule to plan for the worst. Dwell time statistics are often unknown or incorrect.	Verified. When the dwell time perceived as "normal" is higher than the actual dwell time (Kenya, Nigeria), shippers are likely to exert pressure to shorten it; if the perceived dwell time is higher than the actual dwell time (South Africa, Uganda, Zambia), there might be no pressure to shorten it. Communicating reliable information about dwell time is key to avoid ill-adapted strategies and stimulate time performance of customs brokers.

Source: Authors based on firm surveys.

issues, such as the impact of market structure on pricing strategies, should be investigated further.

More analysis could be done with regard to the market structure of the private sector and the role of formal and informal behavior. However, such a study would undoubtedly encounter even greater reluctance on the part of respondents to answer questions that they view as confidential and even greater lack of understanding of the issues.

Notes

1. Appendix B presents a thorough description of the model used and theoretical behaviors.

2. Estimation based on average monthly storage costs for consumer goods, gleaned from local interviews. The currency is the franc Communauté Financière Africaine (FCFA).

3. The calculations are based on a net mass of 30 tons per TEU (20-foot equivalent unit) and a cargo value of US$18,735 per TEU for 2009 (Cameroon customs database).

4. Data do not capture Zambian importers using Dar es Salaam port. Therefore, no comparison is possible in this regard.

5. For descriptive statistics on firms' surveys, see appendix C.

6. In Kenya, pilot surveys were conducted in order to check whether the questions were understood by the interviewees and the length of the questionnaire.

7. This measures the proportion of containerized imports with a dwell time of 0–5 days, 6–10 days, 11–20 days, 21–40 days, 41–70 days, and more than 70 days.

8. All t-tests in this chapter are run on groups with unequal variances; thus Satterthwaite's approximation is computed instead of the usual degree of freedom.

9. This also holds when comparing average dwell time of each category of competitors with the next highest category: shippers that do not have competitors have a three-day shorter dwell time than those that have more than 1 competitor ($t(14.426) = 4.346$; $p = 0.0003$); shippers that face one competitor experience a three-day shorter dwell time than those that have more than two competitors ($t(10.568) = 2.735$; $p = 0.01$); and shippers with two to five competitors have a one-day shorter dwell time than shippers with more than five competitors ($t(150.772) = 1.749$; $p = 0.041$).

10. We use 11 categories based on the 15 standard categories (using two-digit Harmonized System codes). We aggregate some of the categories because

they are too small, but some still account for less than 5 percent of the total volume of imports. This might explain the problem of selection bias.

Reference

Refas, Salim, and Thomas Cantens. 2011. "Why Does Cargo Spend Weeks in African Ports? The Case of Douala, Cameroon." Policy Research Working Paper 5565, World Bank, Washington, DC.

CHAPTER 5

Estimated Impacts and Political Economy of Long Dwell Times

We now analyze the indirect and extended impacts of long dwell times, which are not negligible, especially for the consumer (figure 5.1).

Indirect Impact

The indirect impact of long dwell times, defined as the impact on other containers stored in the yard, can be measured in terms of service time (yard productivity) and truck turnaround time (gate productivity). Long container dwell times increase the congestion factor (defined as the ratio of waiting time to service time) and generate additional idle time in the physical handling of operations. At the same time, high occupancy rates hamper rehandling productivity because they lead to higher storage density and stacking heights and thus longer delays in delivery.

Indirect congestion costs are difficult to measure. We need to estimate, for example, precisely what increase in unit service time is strictly imputable to higher capacity utilization and what is imputable to other factors, such as shift or equipment productivity. In addition, in a multiple-stage process such as port clearance, serial queuing occurs, and congestion at one stage can have a serial effect on other stages.

Figure 5.1   Summary of Main Negative Impacts of Long Container Dwell Times in Sub-Saharan African Ports

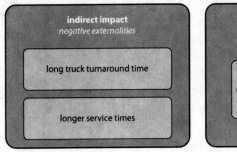

Source: Authors.

Berth Congestion

We start by applying the widely used queuing models to estimate the impact of long dwell times on berth queuing. Queuing models are generally defined using an $X/Y/n$ notation, where X denotes the arrival profile, Y denotes the departure profile, and n denotes the number of service channels. Models used in the port literature generally assume that berths are identical and that a homogeneous fleet of ships calls in the port on a first-come, first-served basis (Fourgeaud n.d.). The pattern of arrival and the distribution of service times are often simulated using an implicit statistical law called Erlang distribution, starting from the basic random distribution (Erlang 1) and moving to increasingly regular ones (Erlang 2, 3...). Using the E2/E2/2 queuing model, for example, in a two-berth port, the congestion factor simulated with an average occupancy rate of 70 percent would be 41 percent, meaning that the average berth waiting time represents about 41 percent of the average berth service time.

Yard Congestion

Other patterns of congestion are also evident at the yard level, and these patterns have received little academic attention. Nevertheless, high occupancy creates congestion effects and eventually affects the service time of containers. We can model these effects using the theory of highway congestion, with service time in port being the equivalent of travel time on highways. Highway congestion models of the following form have been developed with the objective of estimating congestion factors caused by heavy traffic, and they can be used in a similar manner in port congestion analysis (see Sanders, Verhaeghe, and Dekker 2005 for similar work). The equation of service time is of the following form:

$$t = t_{ff}\left(1 + b\left(\tfrac{N}{K}\right)^k\right),$$ (5.1)

where t_{ff} is free-flow service time, N is traffic volume, K is design capacity, and b, k are parameters. If we assume, for example, a "free-flow service time" of about 120 minutes (truck movements, reachstacker movements, container handling, and stiffing) and an occupancy rate of 90 percent,[1] service time would peak at 194 minutes as a result of high occupancy. The additional service time as a result of long dwell times is therefore estimated at 74 minutes per container transiting through the yard.

To convert this congestion effect into monetary terms, we again use an estimate of average daily cargo opportunity cost of FCFA 50,000, and the resulting indirect congestion effect is of FCFA 2,570 per container in the yard.

Rehandling and Final Delivery Costs

An additional indirect cost of high dwell times is the rehandling cost caused by higher yard occupancy rates. When yard occupancy increases, stacking height and storage density also increase and the delivery of containers onto trucks may require additional moves. In an attempt to estimate this number of additional rehandles, Huynh (2006) distinguishes between two stacking configurations: nonmixed storage and mixed storage.[2] In a high-occupancy context, the terminal operator has no choice but to adopt mixed storage with stacking heights of three to four containers or higher. The increasing container dwell times result in a sharp decrease in rehandling productivity that is all the more significant because containers at the bottom of each stack are more likely to be scheduled for delivery first. Using Huynh's model, there would be an average of three rehandles for each delivery in congested Sub-Saharan African ports, which would have a substantial impact on both cost to the operator and truck turnaround time. Cost to the operator can be estimated as half of the handling cost charged to the client (average FCFA 27,500 observed in the ports studied), while the impact on truck turnaround time alone is quite significant (two daily rotations of a truck between the city and the port instead of three), resulting in higher delivery costs.[3] Therefore, we estimate that because of these rehandling issues and longer servicing times, rehandling costs of about FCFA 13,750 are charged to the client, while the truck deliveries per container are 33 percent higher, with a corresponding cost of about FCFA 42,900 per container.[4]

Aggregate Indirect Impact of Long Cargo Dwell Times in the Port of Douala

Our estimate of the aggregate indirect impact of long cargo dwell times in Douala is FCFA 68,019 per container—that is, an average 0.7 percent of cargo value or approximately one–quarter of port charges at Douala (table 5.1).

Trade and Welfare Impact

Beyond cost considerations, longer dwell times also have consequences for trade and welfare. Long dwell times can first be treated as a technical barrier to trade because of the additional cost of imports and exports. USAID (2004), for example, estimates this cost to be US$18 per 20-foot equivalent unit (TEU) for the port of Puerto Limón, Costa Rica, and computes an additional tariff of 0.517 percent on container imports and exports. A general equilibrium model is then used to aggregate the impact of this tariff on the whole Central American region; the net welfare impact that would result from a reduction in dwell time in the port of Puerto Limón is estimated to be US$76.5 million annually.

The net welfare impact is therefore treated as the combination of two factors: an additional cost on imports (equivalent to a tariff increase) and a subsequent reduction in trade volume. We treat these two effects separately. We estimate the additional cost on imports in the two previous sections (direct and indirect cost effects). To measure the impact of long cargo dwell times on trade volume, we now estimate (a) the impact of

Table 5.1   Indirect Effects of Long Cargo Dwell Times on Other Containers Stored in the Yard of Douala Port

Indirect effect	Estimated cost (FCFA)	% of cargo value
Berth congestion	22,550	n.a.
Yard congestion	2,569	n.a.
Rehandling	13,750	n.a.
Truck delivery	42,900	n.a.
Total per container	68,019	n.a.
% of cargo value	n.a.	0.7

Source: Authors.
Note: n.a. = Not applicable.

long dwell times on prices, (b) the price elasticity of demand, and (c) the net loss in volume that is a consequence of both factors.

Impact of High Dwell Times on Prices

The impact of high dwell times on prices depends on the competitive context in which firms operate. In the case of monopolistic or oligopolistic companies that operate as price setters, the increase in factory prices as a result of longer dwell times may be fully reflected in final prices, with a limited impact on market share. The conclusion is, however, different in the case of price-taking companies in perfect competition, where market players refrain from increasing prices even if logistics costs are higher because they are afraid of losing market share to their competitors. These considerations of the short-term impact of long dwell times do not prevent us from assuming that higher dwell times inevitably result in upward pressure on prices in the medium term. Market players would eventually reflect the full logistics costs of products in their final prices. We assume, therefore, that in all situations considered, the perceived cost of long dwell times is fully reflected in final prices.[5]

Price Elasticity of Demand

To derive the impact of additional logistics costs on trade volume, we now estimate the price elasticity of demand. Scarce data are available on the price elasticity of demand in Sub-Saharan African economies. Agbola (2003), using household surveys conducted in South Africa, concludes that price elasticity would be in the range of 0.67–1.25 for food products. In their review of the literature on trade policy in South Africa, Edwards, Cassim, and Seventer (2009) find that estimated aggregate import price elasticities range from −0.53 to −1.04 and update these studies using cointegration analysis with quarterly data from 1962 through 2004. They include a measure of tariff protection, using collection duties, in the import demand function and control for the effect of domestic income and import prices relative to domestic producer prices. Their estimates indicate a long-run import price elasticity of −0.98. Unfortunately, little similar work has been performed for other Sub-Saharan African countries, and therefore, we use this value as a conservative estimate of the price elasticity of demand in lower-income African countries.

A representative value of average dwell times in Sub-Saharan African ports is 20 days. Using FCFA 9.37 million as the average value of cargo and assuming that additional costs are fully reflected in final prices, as discussed in the previous section, long dwell times therefore lead to an estimated price increase of about 10.3 percent in our example. In addition, there is an extra indirect cost of about 0.7 percent. In total, the price increase due to long dwell times is estimated as 11 percent of the market price. Given the price elasticity of demand of 0.98, assumed above, we can therefore broadly estimate that long cargo dwell times in a typical Sub-Saharan African port would lead to an average decrease of about 10.78 percent in the aggregate demand for imports of containerized cargo in Sub-Saharan African countries. This is a pure loss to the economy.

Containers account for about half of the total volume of imports in Sub-Saharan African countries (UNCTAD 2009). The net welfare loss to the economy of 20 days average container dwell time in Sub-Saharan African ports, as opposed to average dwell times shorter than seven days in most developed economies, is therefore considered equivalent to the net welfare loss that would result from a 5.39 percent reduction in the volume of total imports. This loss is estimated in monetary terms as the net difference between market prices and consumer willingness to pay (consumer surplus) and market prices and purchasing costs (trader surplus). Market prices only tell us the minimum amount that people who buy the good would be willing to pay for it; in practice, the economic benefit they get from buying the good is higher. Accordingly, traders benefit from their sales by applying a markup to their purchasing cost.

It is challenging to estimate losses in both consumer surplus and producer surplus resulting from a 5.39 percent decrease in total imports without having actual information on products and markets. Nevertheless, it is possible to conclude that the net welfare loss to the economy accrues to a significant portion of the market value of the total imports of a country.[6]

The Political Economy of Dwell Time in Sub-Saharan Africa

If we exclude Durban and, to a lesser extent, Mombasa, most ports in Sub-Saharan Africa have average cargo dwell times of longer than 15 days (compared to three to four days in most large international ports).

The main findings of the previous chapters demonstrate that the level of professionalism of importers and clearing and forwarding (C&F) agents and the strategies of shippers have a major impact on cargo dwell time.

Even more important, market structure of the private sector explains the hysteresis of cargo dwell time. For instance, C&F concentration has two main adverse effects on dwell times: (a) the weak negotiating power of clients with these main C&F agents, which leads to a low level of service, and (b) the development of low-cost unprofessional C&F agents who have no choice but to compete for the rest of the market on price at the expense of quality.

Firm analysis and case studies have also demonstrated that low competency and cash constraints explain why most importers do not seek to reduce cargo dwell time because, in most cases, doing so would increase their input costs. Moreover, monopolists-cartels may have a stronger incentive to reduce cargo dwell time, but the goal is to maximize profit (and not to adjust prices downward).

Most ports in Sub-Saharan Africa suffer from a vicious circle in which long cargo dwell time (two to three weeks) benefits the stakeholders and constitutes a strong barrier to entry in global markets. It also explains why most industries, which are not time-sensitive, such as exports of raw materials or minerals, prosper and why time-sensitive ones (those that add value) do not.

This also explains why cargo dwell times have not declined substantially for years: the pressure from the private sector is not real in most cases and enables some importers to remain competitive by avoiding worldwide competition. It could also explain why most trade facilitation measures, such as community-based systems in ports, have faced so many difficulties in implementation in Sub-Saharan Africa. Transparency in this environment is synonymous with reducing multiple rents and increasing real competition. There is then a coalition of interests in favor of the status quo; unless some practices are amended in the public and private sectors, long cargo dwell time and lack of assembling trade will persist.

Moreover, terminal operators may have incentives that also affect dwell time. Given that storage tariffs generate revenue for the port operator, the optimal policy could be to increase dwell time for terminal operators in Sub-Saharan Africa, especially when there is no congestion.

Finally, in a competitive environment, port authorities want to reduce dwell times and increase the overall efficiency of port operations for attracting more traffic. However, port authorities might be interested in increasing dwell times for the following reasons: (a) because employees receive informal payments as total revenues in the port increase and (b) longer dwell time provides an excellent justification for increasing port capacity, which means additional funding for infrastructure investments (all the more if donors are ready to finance infrastructure investments). In this context, importers, terminal operators, and port authorities do not have a strong incentive to reduce cargo dwell time.

The potential number of actors who may drive change both in private industry and in the logistics business is therefore much lower than generally anticipated, all the more so because the adjustments (including for these potential allies) are significant and do not guarantee an impact, as all players need to contribute for any system to yield results.

Notes

1. Yard occupancy rate observed, for example, in Douala in October 2010.
2. In nonmixed storage, every containership load is stored separately in the terminal; in mixed storage, new containers can be stacked on top of containers already stored in the yard. Nonmixed storage is generally more efficient.
3. Handling costs are set by the concession agreement and cannot be increased, regardless of the additional number of rehandles (interviews with trucking companies in Douala, October 2010).
4. FCFA is the franc Communauté Financière Africaine. This is 5 percent of the median delivery cost in the Douala area, where delivery costs range between FCFA 100,000 and FCFA 160,000 (according to delivery zone).
5. Perceived cost is computed as the sum of parking fees and demurrage charges. Field investigation has confirmed that most shippers have only a limited knowledge of their full inventory costs and calculate factory prices on the basis of purchasing costs, production costs, and direct transport and clearance charges. Neither inventory costs nor opportunity costs are fully valued.
6. Sub-Saharan African markets are generally not competitive because of supplier concentration, so producer surplus alone is expected to be superior to 10 percent of the corresponding value, that is, about 0.5 percent of the total value of imports to the country.

References

Agbola, F. W. 2003. "Estimation of Food Demand Patterns in South Africa Based on a Survey of Households." *Journal of Agricultural and Applied Economics* 35 (3): 662–67.

Edwards, Lawrence, Rashad Cassim, and Dirk Van Seventer. 2009. "Trade Policy since Democracy." In *South African Economic Policy under Democracy*, ed. Janine Aron, Brian Kahn, and Geeta Kingdon. Oxford, U.K.: Oxford University Press.

Fourgeaud, Patrick. n.d. "Measuring Port Performance." World Bank, Washington, DC. http://siteresources.worldbank.org/INTPRAL/Resources/338897-111 7630103824/fourgeau.pdf.

Huynh, Nathan. 2006. "Boosting Marine Container Terminals Throughput: A Survey of Strategies." Paper 06-2744, presented at the annual meeting of the Transportation Research Board, Washington, DC, January.

Sanders, F. M., R. J. Verhaeghe, and S. Dekker. 2005. "Investment Dynamics for a Congested Transport Network with Competition: Application to Port Planning." Paper presented at the 23rd international conference of the System Dynamics Society, July 17–21, Boston. www.systemdynamics.org.

UNCTAD (United Nations Conference on Trade and Development). 2009. *Review of Maritime Transport*. New York: UNCTAD Secretariat. http://www .unctad.org.

USAID (U.S. Agency for International Development). 2004. *The Broad Economic Impact of Port Inefficiency: A Comparative Study of Two Ports*. Washington, DC: USAID. http://pdf.usaid.gov/pdf_docs/PNADC612.pdf.

CHAPTER 6

Policy Recommendations to Reduce Dwell Time

This chapter presents the main traditional and nontraditional measures that should be undertaken to reduce dwell time, especially in an environment characterized by poor governance.

Figures Matter: What Should Be Measured by Whom and What Should Be the Target?

Dwell time figures are a major commercial instrument used to attract cargo and generate revenues. Therefore, the incentives for port authorities and container terminal operators are increasingly strong to lower the real figure. For this reason, at a time when ports are more and more in competition, the question of how to obtain independently verifiable dwell time data is increasingly critical to provide assurance that interventions are having the intended effect.

With the proliferation of off-dock container yards (ODCYs) in Sub-Saharan Africa, the number of containers is growing, and, in several countries, those that exit the port yard are then dropped from the dwell time statistics published by port authorities or container terminals. However, from a trade perspective, as long as a container has not been cleared, dwell time continues to increase. Moreover, in some cases, there are pressures to start dwell time when the last container is discharged from a vessel, which can translate into a three- to four-day difference between dwell time for the first and last containers discharged.

Port authorities or container terminal operators generally have published data on dwell time, but it is becoming increasingly important to cross-check published data to understand the methodology used to compile them and judge their reliability. In this context, as the example of Douala demonstrates, the best and most reliable data are customs data. Donors need to obtain access to customs databases if they are going to address dwell time issues,[1] because, unlike port authorities and terminal operators, customs agencies do not have a strong incentive to report shorter dwell times.

In this regard, with the assistance of the World Bank, the Dar es Salaam corridor is developing a transport observatory that will attempt to measure and report dwell time automatically, including dwell time for containers held at ODCYs.

Average or mean dwell time has usually been the main target indicator in Sub-Saharan Africa. It has the advantage of being easy to compute and easy to understand. However, because a quarter of shipments have extremely long dwell time, average or mean dwell time can hardly decrease in the short or medium term. Douala, for example, set an objective of seven days at the end of the 1990s but still experiences dwell times of more than 18 days, despite the improvements made by some shippers.

Despite its weaknesses, average or mean dwell time captures the share of problematic shipments and is a proxy for governance problems (with regard to customs auctions and abandoned cargo). Therefore, this indicator should not be dropped completely.

But a second indicator should be developed for efficient shippers in Sub-Saharan African ports: dwell time for the first quartile of shipments or the median dwell time. This indicator is more difficult to compute because it requires having access to shipment data, but it would be more reliable than average dwell time and would be helpful for assessing the impact of public policy interventions. In our case studies, mean time would be nine days in Dar es Salaam, 14 days in Douala, and three days in Durban; the first quartile target would be four days for Dar es Salaam and eight days for Douala.

The Importance of a Sensitization Campaign

The findings from firm surveys and political economy analysis indicate that most measures, starting with building more storage capacity, often do not have the expected positive impact on dwell time. A public information campaign is needed to disseminate findings on the main causes of long dwell times. In most cases, the perceived causes, such as lack of terminal capacity, do not hold, and structural issues need to be addressed. Even if investments were made, without structural changes, dwell time would probably remain the same.

The Usual Measures and Their Limits

The usual measures undertaken to reduce port dwell time are relatively limited in number and are summarized in table 6.1. These techniques have different impacts on different segments of the distribution function and thus affect shippers in different ways. An increase in prearrival processing would have less impact on cargo with long dwell time, for example. What

Table 6.1   The Usual Measures to Reduce Port Dwell Time

Indicator	Measure
Operational dwell time	
Transfer to ODCY	Transfer cargo to ODCY
Infrastructure investment	Invest in infrastructure (quays, berths)
Equipment investment	Invest in equipment (cranes, reachstackers, software)
Transactional dwell time	
Prearrival processing	Submit documentation prior to arrival of vessel and decide on required clearance procedure
Document review	Reduce the additional documentation required when reviewing the declaration and supporting documentation
Inspection levels	Manage risk, lower the percentage of shipments subject to physical inspection, and improve sampling procedures for shipments subject to physical inspection
Post-clearance inspection	Delay inspection procedures until after the shipment has left the port, including post-clearance audit
Cargo auction	Reduce time before long-term cargo is auctioned
Storage	
Free time	Reduce free time
Rates	Increase the level of charges for each period
Rate escalation	Increase the frequency of escalation of charges

Source: Authors.

matters most are measures that seek to change the incentives of key stake-holders, especially shippers.

Off-Dock Storage

In recent years, ODCYs have been developed in the major ports in Sub-Saharan Africa. In Mombasa, the main strategy for overcoming the excess demand for storage has been to introduce a set of ODCYs (otherwise referred to as container freight stations or CFSs). This effort began in October 2007, with the introduction of two facilities.[2] In Tema, the development of the current system of off-dock container yards began in 2007, with the opening of the Golden Jubilee Terminal under the control of the Ghana Ports and Harbours Authority (GPHA). This was followed by the opening of four private terminals. The ODCYs operate on a one-year license and pay a royalty to the GPHA. The shipping lines, in consultation with the GPHA, decide whether to transfer the containers to the ODCY.

Dar es Salaam developed a network of 10 ODCYs to provide overflow capacity for the container terminal. The introduction of the ODCYs increased the available storage capacity, reducing some of the bottlenecks associated with congestion.[3] However, despite a more efficient arrangement for storing and clearing containers, dwell time has not dropped significantly.[4] The new system creates space in the port yard. However, unless it is coupled with other measures—a reduction in customs clearance time, for instance—the system will not decrease total dwell time and could eventually increase it, if the CFS owner is allowed to charge additional storage fees.[5]

Tariffs and Port Pricing

Pricing at a port and other links along the logistics chain can create incentives to delay cargo and prolong its stay in port.[6] Key components of price and cost can affect behaviors and financial decisions of importers, exporters, and shipping agencies, including the following: (a) various types of port tariffs associated with specific services—vessel services, cargo handling, and storage, (b) financial costs to be paid to the banks to manage debt, (c) prices of storage services both inside and outside a port, and (d) other practices with financial consequences, such as customs auctions.

Port pricing is based on a mix of pricing strategies designed to reflect the demand for port services, the competition between ports, and the cost of providing the services. Demand-based pricing strategies are used when there is little competition; they measure demand according to the port user's ability to pay and the benefits derived from using the port's resources. Prices based on competition involve a rate comparison between charges in competing ports (or possibly a comparison of user costs based on the quality of service) and generalized costs involving distance, time, and inventory costs (Arnold 1985).

One of the most straightforward incentives for importers to delay cargo shipment is berth and storage tariffs, which are lower than other opportunity costs. This situation is particularly relevant to small importers, who do not own a streamlined supply chain that connects to retailers or end customers and prefer to sell to buyers directly from the vessel. In such a case, there are two options. First, the importer can move the cargo to an intermediate storage area (outside a port) at a total cost of cargo-handling fees, customs duties, value added tax, and storage fees. Second, the importer can leave cargo in the port either on berth or in storage at a total cost of berth tariffs or port storage tariffs multiplied by the number of days, subtracting financial gain obtained from delaying the payments enumerated in the first alterative. When port tariffs are too cheap to incentivize prompt shipment from ports, as is often the case in Sub-Saharan Africa, importers will choose the second option.

An increase in rates combined with an increase in the frequency of their escalation would not affect the consignees who clear their cargo in the free time period but would encourage consignees experiencing delays due to coordination problems to reduce their dwell time. The impact would be more dramatic on those consignees who use the port to manage their inventory, especially those who have to locate a buyer for their cargo. However, the rate increase would increase the proportion of long-stay cargo that is abandoned.

The standard tariff for storing import containers in the terminal includes a free time period that corresponds to the minimum dwell time for a reasonably efficient consignee. This minimum dwell time is three to five days in ports with efficient operations and border control procedures, but seven to 10 days in ports with inefficient operations and procedures. Following the free period, a fixed daily charge is levied. The rate escalates at intervals in order to discourage consignees from using the terminal for long-term storage. A common interval is seven to 10 days (figure 6.1).

In Sub-Saharan Africa, a third component has been introduced to address the reluctance of consignees to pay for double handling. This is a long-stay charge levied at the end of the free time. It offsets any savings in handling costs that might be realized by keeping cargo in the terminal.

As long as the free time period is adequate, the terminal operator is not taking advantage of a monopoly position when setting the tariff. Instead,

Figure 6.1   Storage Charges, by Number of Days in Container Yard

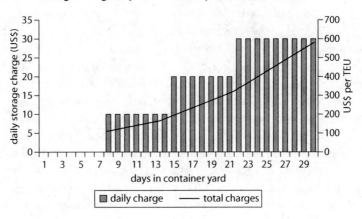

Source: Authors.
Note: TEU = 20-foot equivalent unit.

it prices storage in the port container yard to compete with private storage outside the port. If the price is too high, the yard will be relatively empty. If it is too low, the yard will be congested. With a reasonable tariff, most of the revenue will be obtained from cargo that is removed during the seven to 10 days immediately following the free time period.

The adjustment of storage tariffs in order to avoid congestion can take one of three forms: a reduction in free time, an increase in daily rates, and a reduction in the time between rate increases. An example of each form is shown in figure 6.2. Initially, the free time period is reduced from 10 days to five. Next, rates are doubled. Finally, the frequency of escalation is reduced from two weeks to one week. The resulting rise in charges as a function of days in storage is dramatic, as shown in figure 6.3.

In this regard, Durban is probably the best example in Sub-Saharan Africa. Transnet Port Terminals explained that to achieve its target dwell time of three days, one of the more practical and simple measures employed was to enforce terms and conditions related to the storage of cargo at ports. These conditions state that, within 72 hours of discharging each container from the vessel, the customer or the container operator must provide the terminal operator with delivery instructions for all containers discharged. All containers remaining after the 72-hour period has expired will incur storage charges, as shown in table 6.2. Charges for Durban are almost six times higher than for other ports in the country.

Uncleared cargo or cargo detained by customs for inspection is moved to a licensed container depot either by the carrier or by the terminal

Figure 6.2   Tariff Adjustments, by Number of Days in Storage

Figure 6.3   Cumulative Storage Charges, by Number of Days in Storage

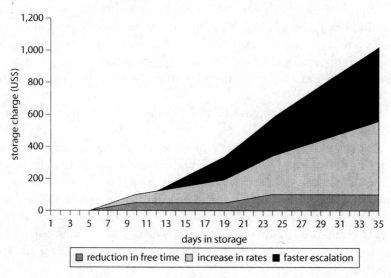

Source: Authors.

Table 6.2   Storage Fees for Import Containers in Durban Port, 2011
US$ per unit (estimated)

Number of days in storage	6 meters per 20-foot equivalent unit	12 meters per 40-foot equivalent unit
Days 1–3	Free	Free
Day 4	90	181
Day 5	237	475
Day 6	477	954
Day 7	716	1,432
Day 8	956	1,911
Day 9	1,195	2,389
Day 10	1,435	2,867

Source: Transnet Port Terminals.

operator. Licensed depots generally provide cheaper storage than the terminal. About 90 percent of cargo can and is generally cleared within three days, and less than 10 percent of cargo is moved to a bonded warehouse, where the average stay is estimated at around seven to eight days and less than 1 percent ends up as long-stay or abandoned cargo (that is, 28 days or more) that then goes to state auction. Free storage for transshipments is seven days, but given the small proportions, Transnet Port Terminals does not seem too concerned, unlike most cargo handlers.

Among major stakeholders, the introduction of the "penalty storage" fee after day three is probably the most important single event affecting dwell time at Durban port. Even though it took some months for the impact to materialize, Durban Container Terminal saw a continuous drop in dwell time and a reduction in the number of import containers in yard at any given time.

Such port storage charges lead to a virtuous circle for cargo dwell time (figure 6.4).

Durban was able to improve dwell time because systems were in place to allow for prompt clearance and release as well as pre-clearance. The length of dwell time before the increase in port tariffs was due to the low price of port storage, which was approximately US$10 per 20-foot equivalent unit (TEU) per day, often cheaper than taking delivery if commercial storage was required. For this to work, the terminal has to perceive itself as part of a logistics chain and not as a storage facility.

Other African ports have used the same approach, but with a smaller positive impact. In Mombasa, storage charges were doubled in February 2008 in order to address the problem of congestion in the container yard,

Figure 6.4   The Virtuous Circle of Cargo Dwell Time

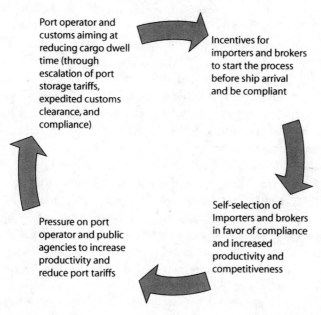

Port operator and customs aiming at reducing cargo dwell time (through escalation of port storage tariffs, expedited customs clearance, and compliance)

Incentives for importers and brokers to start the process before ship arrival and be compliant

Self-selection of Importers and brokers in favor of compliance and increased productivity and competitiveness

Pressure on port operator and public agencies to increase productivity and reduce port tariffs

Source: Authors.

but the impact on dwell time was minimal. In October 2009, the free time for containers stored in the port terminal was reduced from seven to five days for domestic imports and from 15 to 11 days for transit imports. But the impact was modest. In Tema, storage rates and free time period were also adjusted in 2008. Free time was increased from five to seven days, but this had little impact on dwell time.[7] In Dar es Salaam, the container terminal tariff was modified in August 2009. Free time was reduced from 10 calendar days to seven for imports, but remained at 15 calendar days for transit cargo. Storage charges were doubled. Subsequently, a late clearance fee was introduced to encourage consignees to clear cargo within the free time period. This was supposed to encourage importers to remove their cargo more rapidly, but the impact was marginal and difficult to determine. The increase in port tariffs and reduction in free time as well as the rationalization of charges for moving cargo to the ODCYs provided an incentive to reduce time spent in storage but had a relatively small impact on dwell time, in part because the contribution of storage charges to delivered cost is small, especially for transit cargo.

In Lomé, it is even worse. The port of Lomé operates in a competitive environment (competition from Tema and Cotonou for the hinterland countries) and has long opted for competitive pricing policies. After the free time period has expired, tariff bands are charged as follows: FCFA 678, FCFA 1,356, and FCFA 2,715 (equivalent to less than US$10), which are much lower than tariffs charged by other ports in the subregion. Lomé's free time policy favors transiting cargo, with a free time period of only four days for domestic traffic and 21 days for transiting goods. The Port Authority of Lomé seems reluctant to use pricing to lower dwell time for fear of losing competitive advantage over other ports.

Tariff changes may have a limited impact on dwell time in an environment with poor governance due to three reasons: (a) the combination of taxes, duties, and escalating storage charges can cause shippers who have problems with cash flow or are unable to find a buyer to abandon their cargo after a month, (b) cargo staying longer than one month often does not pay the full storage charges; the consignee negotiates a significant discount (and probably a discount on other duties as well) as part of an agreement to remove the cargo; and (c) terminal operators, who obtain a significant increase in income from storage charges, do not necessarily want dwell time to decrease.

In conclusion, in Lomé port, low tariffs are a disincentive to reducing dwell time and should be discouraged (even though low tariffs probably explain why traffic has grown in the recent years). Moreover, a free time period of seven days seems reasonable in the African context (for domestic and transit cargo); a limit on the free time period should be coupled with an escalation of tariffs of several dozen dollars a day, but not to the extent seen in Durban, which is probably not replicable in many Sub-Saharan African countries.

Experiences from Recent Successful Initiatives

Two ports, Dar es Salaam and Durban, have achieved noticeable improvements in the last decade, based on (a) political impetus from the top of the state, (b) regular meetings of stakeholders at a decision-making level, (c) audit teams to reengineer processes, and (d) a comprehensive approach to changing the behavior of stakeholders. All of these components seem to be necessary ingredients of a durable reduction in dwell time.

The Importance of Regular Meetings of Stakeholders at the Decision-Making Level

The first example in Sub-Saharan Africa comes from Durban port. Average dwell time was around seven days in 2002 (and was reduced to three days in 2004). Following recurrent mutual complaints between Transnet Port Terminals and private stakeholders on dwell time and its causes, an interim advisory board was created, co-chaired by a manager from Transnet and a chief executive officer from the private sector, with the mandate to identify the key measures that should be implemented to reduce dwell time. Over a period of three years, this committee met fortnightly. Its composition is described in figure 6.5.

An audit team was added to the group to provide an independent view on what should be done. This team was commissioned on an ad hoc basis to give technical advice on the measures to be taken. It was composed of a representative of a shipping line, a representative of the road freight association, a representative of Portnet, and a representative of an engineering firm.

The lessons from Durban show that the terminal operator first needs to reengineer its internal processes and procedures and then to agree on measures to change the behavior of private stakeholders, such as shipping lines, transporters, customs brokers, and so on.

It is also critical to resolve high-impact problems first and then to agree with port users on the problem to be resolved. In this regard, it is important to demonstrate that dwell time can be reduced. Durban stakeholders used a comprehensive "enabling block" approach (figure 6.6), which changed the incentives for crane operators, changed port tariffs, altered the opening hours of container yard operators, established a queuing system for trucks, and invested in software and equipment.

In Dar es Salaam in June 2008, a multistakeholder workshop on dwell time identified 205 issues and proposed actions to improve the performance of dwell time. The process was championed by high-level intervention by the president and prime minister, which resulted in the formation of a multistakeholder Port Decongestion Committee, which met fortnightly.

Moreover, stakeholders commissioned a committee of specialists to identify key measures to reduce dwell time. The setup and functioning of the Port Improvement Committee (PIC) is similar to the approach taken in Durban. For example, participation is at the chief executive level, both private and public sector agencies are represented, meetings are held fortnightly, and two subcommittees—one on dwell time and another on standard operating procedures—convene to tackle specific technical assignments on behalf of the PIC. The subcommittee on procedures undertakes audits on choke points in any area of port operations.

It took about one year to develop the strategy for increasing storage throughput and altering the behavior of the various participants. Out of

Figure 6.5   Institutional Structure of the Interim Advisory Board in Durban Port

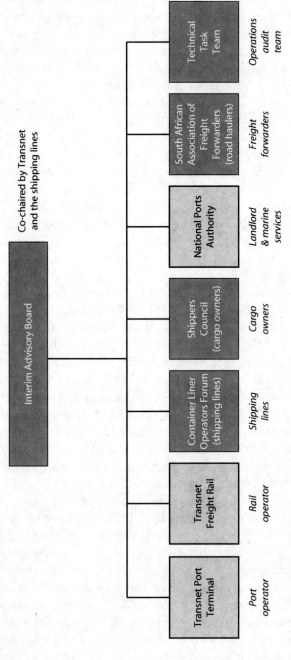

Source: SACTAB files 2002, Transnet Africa.

Figure 6.6   Enabling Block Strategy to Reduce Dwell Time in Durban Port

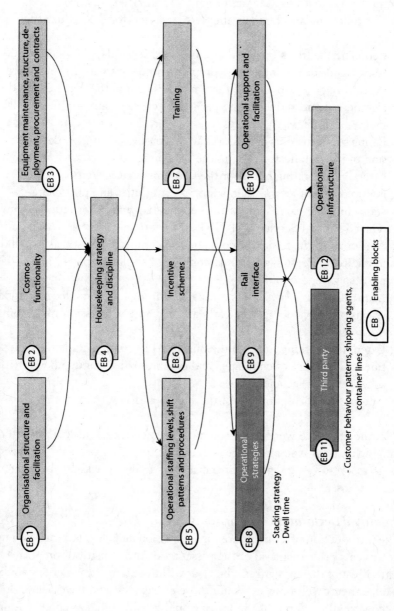

- Stacking strategy
- Dwell time

- Customer behaviour patterns, shipping agents,
  container lines

EB Enabling blocks

EB 1 Organisational structure and facilitation

EB 2 Cosmos functionality

EB 3 Equipment maintenance, structure, deployment, procurement and contracts

EB 4 Housekeeping strategy and discipline

EB 5 Operational staffing levels, shift patterns and procedures

EB 6 Incentive schemes

EB 7 Training

EB 8 Operational strategies

EB 9 Rail interface

EB 10 Operational support and facilitation

EB 11 Third party

EB 12 Operational infrastructure

Source: SACTAB files 2002, Transnet Africa.

205 issues identified through stakeholder consultations, the PIC summarized 10 priority actions to reduce dwell time and improve productivity in the port. Reports by the PIC indicate that dwell time was reduced from 25 days to 15 in 2009 and then to 13 in 2010.

The following are the main measures credited for this reduction:[8]

- Reducing the free storage period to 15 and seven days, respectively, for transit and local containers, complemented by two other measures: introducing a punitive tariff for containers kept in the port beyond the free period and reducing the period for customs auction of undocumented containers to 21 days
- Easing some customs procedures, for example, allowing partial submission of the manifest, reducing the percentage of physical inspections, extending operating hours for the Customs Service Center, and speeding up payment arrangements for customs duties and port charges
- Canceling the exclusivity clause of the Tanzania International Container Terminal Services (TICTS) contract to allow the Tanzania Ports Authority (TPA) to handle containers in competition with TICTS and, in addition, creating additional container-handling capacity inside the port (space and equipment)
- Launching public awareness campaigns through print media, radio, and television to encourage the early and accurate submission of customs documents
- Extending working hours in the port to 24 hours to include the collection and delivery of containers and synchronizing working hours with other relevant agencies
- Automating the operations of the TICTS and TPA.

Although there were noticeable improvements, it is difficult to determine what improvements were attributable to the 20 percent dropoff in cargo as a result of the global financial crisis and what was attributable to the reforms.

Prearrival Declaration and Customs Auction Process

The introduction of a procedure for submission and clearance of customs documents prior to arrival of the vessel reduces the distribution of dwell time. Most of the consignees who clear within the free time period would reduce their dwell time, as would those consignees who have delays due to coordination. Some of the latter would be able to clear goods within the free time period. Most of the consignees who store their containers in the port while arranging to sell the goods would not be affected by this change. The same would apply to long-term cargo. In this regard, incentives to clear cargo before arrival are critical to reduce cargo dwell time.

The role of shipping agents and their interaction with the broker, consignee, and customs may also explain the relatively large delay upstream of the declaration itself. How customs, the shipping line, and the container operator manage the manifest information is a critical component of delay and the primary objective of a single window or port community system.

To reduce long-term cargo dwell time, customs auction practices need to be amended in many countries, and doing so should be at the core of any plan to tackle cargo dwell time. Auctions should be transparent, published in the press and online, and organized after a delay of four to six weeks.

Customs auction practices can indirectly incentivize importers to extend their port dwell time. Cargo owners or importers, who are often unable or unwilling to pay very high duty on their high-value goods, deliberately delay formal procedures to take advantage of customs auction practices. This becomes possible when the auction does not take place according to the procedure. Under the alternative (illegal) auction practice, the importer buys back his own goods at an artificially low price in return for paying a commission to the customs agency.

In Dar es Salaam, the current auction procedure still allows cargo to remain in the port or ODCY for at least a month and a half (one month in Durban, but three months in Douala). It can even be more problematic for government cargo, which is a major component of long-stay cargo in Dar es Salaam.

In this regard, Nigeria offers an even more compelling example (Raballand and Mjekiqi 2010). Abandoned cargo is relatively common in Lagos port. There are two types of cargo abandonment, both of which rely on the repurchase of abandoned goods at auction as a way to bypass normal import fees and procedures:[9]

- An importer abandons prohibited goods in the port and waits for them to be auctioned, at which point he or she bypasses the import regulation and gets the goods at a relatively low price.
- An importer makes a false declaration, including the undervaluation of declared goods. When caught, he or she abandons the consignment and purchases the goods through auction, which is cheaper than paying full import duties, penalties for making a false declaration, and incidental port charges.

The Nigeria Customs Service's liberal auction policy encourages low compliance with import procedures. Indeed, in Lagos port, auctioned goods rarely bring more than US$3,500 for a 40-foot container, even for high-value goods such as some textile products.[10] In 2009, Nigeria Customs Service relaxed the conditions for releasing goods to reduce port congestion. As a customs official explained at the time, "Out of 50 containers that have been examined, only one importer came forward to take delivery of his cargo. In some terminals, no importer whose consignment falls into the category of overtime cargo has shown his face." In the case of prohibited imports, the best option seems to be to let the cargo go to auction and repurchase it at a low price.

Customs auctions have a major impact on dwell time, leading to long dwell times for importers, who take this route to reduce paid tariff duties.

Information technology systems and changes in human resources policies are keys to customs modernization and thus have a major impact on cargo dwell time.

In the port of Durban, the customs modernization project made a significant contribution to improving competitiveness. The strategy of enhanced compliance recognized three key elements influencing customs operations: (a) some taxpayers and traders will always try to comply whether enforcement is effective or not, (b) the goal is to influence the undecided majority who will choose one way or the other based on how well the strategy is implemented, and (c) some taxpayers or traders—criminals—will not comply whether enforcement is effective or not.

Within that context, the strategy was based on the fundamental principles of making it easy for those trying to comply by improving services and making it hard for those not wanting to comply by improving enforcement. Therefore, measures were initiated to increase treatment differentiation and compliance.

The target for the South African Revenue Services (SARS) is to clear declarations processed through Electronic Data Interchange (EDI) within three hours. According to SARS, during the first quarter of 2011, the average time to release goods was three hours when processed through EDI and 10 hours when not processed through EDI (with 75 percent of declarations processed through EDI). At the port of Durban, with customs clearing cargo in less than one day and Transnet Port Terminals moving cargo efficiently from the terminal, there is no "transactional dwell time" at the port of Durban, according to one stakeholder (or at least it is rather limited).

In this regard, contractualization between customs brokers and customs was developed. For instance, companies wishing to become an authorized economic operator needed to go through detailed interviews and be transparent regarding their economic activities and supply operations; they are randomly inspected from time to time. However, these companies[11] benefit from a green channel, which means that as soon as the cargo is handled at the port, it can be removed. Contrary to most countries in Sub-Saharan Africa, pre-clearance is the rule, which explains why the target for customs clearance time is in hours and not in days like in other countries.

Contracting in the Port and the Importance of Human Resources Policies

In Durban, a key initiative to altering behavior was the introduction of the Container Terminal Operation Contract (CTOC) with key customers, mainly shipping lines. The CTOC establishes service-level agreements between Transnet Port Terminals and its customers regarding expected levels of performance. These bind the parties by contract to deliver specified targets such as level of service based on agreed performance indicators (that is, a dedicated berthing window, a guarantee of 28 gross crane-hours) on the part of the terminal operator and the observance of specific regulations on the part of private port users (that is, compliance with specific requirements such as providing accurate information).[12] Failure to do so attracts sanctions.

Enforcement of CTOC agreements has been critical for success. Further incentives include a commitment to provide an agreed level of service to specific customers, while the customer commits to clearing cargo from the port within agreed time limits.

Human resources policies are at the core of the reform in South African customs, and Cameroon customs also adopted performance contracts. In 2007, Cameroon customs launched a reform and modernization initiative (Cantens et al. 2011). The reform began with the installation of ASYCUDA (Automated System for Customs Data), a customs clearance system that allows the administration not only to track the processing of each consignment, but also to measure a substantial number of criteria relevant to the reform, such as compliance with the deadline for recording the manifest by consignees. For almost two years, upper management and frontline officers in Cameroon customs shared the same reality thanks to "figures" (performance indicators) that measured how the reforms initiated by the former were applied by the latter. But, while the initial quantification phase bore fruit, its impact later stalled. A possible solution was adopted, beginning in 2010, when Cameroon customs introduced a system of individual performance contracts[13] to measure the actions and behaviors of customs officers operating at two of the seven Douala port bureaus, using indicators extracted from ASYCUDA. The outcomes are encouraging. After more than a year of implementation, the Cameroon customs bureaus in the experimental group showed better results than the control group on indicators related to reduction of corruption, collection of revenue, and facilitation of trade.

In Douala Port I, the duties and taxes assessed over the period increased by 6.2 percent in 2010 relative to 2009, while the number of imported containers fell by 3 percent. The tax yield of the declarations in Office Douala Port I rose by 3 percent over the contract period in 2010 compared to the same period in 2009. In Office Douala Port V, it rose by 23 percent.[14]

The additional revenues generated during the experiment were an estimated US$23.3 million (which is about 3 percent of the national customs revenue target).[15] The impact of the performance contracts on customs clearance time was equally important. The share of declarations assessed by inspectors on the day they were lodged in the system by brokers was multiplied by 1.3 in Office Douala Port I (it is now around 84 percent), by 1.2 in Office Douala Port V (77 percent), and by 0.9 in Office Douala Port VI (57 percent). The estimated gain in terms of clearance time is eight hours for Office Douala Port I and 14 hours for Office Douala Port V.

In Durban, while the process started off with both parties playing the blame game, the partnership between Portnet and its customers appears to be working well, as reflected in the recent Barloworld survey of 2010. At least, more than half of those in the automotive industry proclaim that the logistics capacity of South Africa's ports has improved in the last two years, and they also think that the loading and docking capacity is now competitive and comparable to international practice. The industry also gives customs a vote of confidence by confirming that compliance processes are being dealt with more efficiently than in the past, that corruption has decreased, and that physical security of goods in the port has improved.

Such changes are obviously challenging, but necessary. Without them, Sub-Saharan African countries will continue to remain largely dependent on exporting raw materials and will not be able to increase value added or create sustainable growth. And a country like Cameroon has shown that it is possible, which should encourage more Sub-Saharan African countries.

How Could Donors Help to Reduce Dwell Time?

Above all, donors should highlight the need to improve performance in this area and should help to energize the demand side of the equation— that is, the general public who stands to lose greatly in terms of net welfare loss from the perpetuation of the problem. They should be more transparent on the difference between most ports in Sub-Saharan Africa and the rest of the world, explaining the direct and indirect consequences of poor performance for consumer prices in Sub-Saharan Africa.

In conclusion, donors should help to reduce dwell time by (a) providing technical assistance to benchmark ports using reliable data;[16] (b) providing technical and independent expertise to identify key constraints, ensuring that local efforts are not captured by vested interests, and verifying that the measures being pursued are indeed welfare enhancing; and (c) refraining from supporting investment infrastructure without first trying to support structural reforms to change the behavior of stakeholders.

The last point is probably the most critical because the widespread assumption that an increase in port infrastructure will necessarily translate into reduced dwell time does not hold in the medium to long term, especially with regard to the physical expansion of port premises. Using the example of Durban, we demonstrate that a reduction in dwell time from a week to four days more than doubles the capacity of the container terminal without any investment in physical extensions: when container movements are speeded up, higher throughput is possible, making investments in larger port storage areas unnecessary.

Significant change is needed, including among donors and development partners. Given the current level of dwell time in Sub-Saharan Africa, one of the worst options (yet one that appears "natural" or "logical") is to invest in additional storage and off-dock yards. Indeed, if dwell time is not reduced, after a couple of years, new extensions costing millions of U.S. dollars will be required that would not have been necessary if dwell time had been reduced. Structural factors, such as rents through customs clearance, customs broker inefficiency, and poor handling need to be tackled before investing in physical extensions of storage.

Local populations pay twice for long dwell times: as taxpayers, because most physical extensions and infrastructure are public investments, and as consumers, because inefficiencies and rents in the port are charged to the final user of these services. Such investments in infrastructure tend to strengthen rents and do not tackle structural issues, creating unintended consequences. A typical example is the construction by public operators in landlocked countries of off-dock container yards in port cities, which de facto relieve congestion in the transit port, but would be unnecessary if transit processes were tackled correctly. They only give agents from these landlocked countries an opportunity to charge rents on transit cargo. Such infrastructure, which was built in the 1970s and 1980s and abandoned in the 1990s, has come back in fashion to address congestion in some key ports.

The solution to decrease dwell time in Sub-Saharan Africa for the most part relies on the challenging task of breaking the private sector's collusion and the status quo between public authorities, logistics operators, and some shippers. When facing a capacity shortage, the best option is to reduce dwell time first and only then to consider expanding capacity.

Notes

1. In Dar es Salaam, since goods cannot be permitted to leave a customs-controlled area (port or container freight station) without customs release, the period taken to obtain a customs release gives a fair indication of actual dwell time and is more reliable than port data alone.

2. These were authorized by Kenya Ports Authority, with containers allocated to these facilities through direct nomination on the shipping line manifest.

3. The introduction of ODCY was part of several reforms introduced by the Port Decongestion Committee. Initially, the allocation to individual ODCYs was made based on a daily poll to determine which ODCY had sufficient empty space to receive a full load of import containers. Two restrictions were placed on this procedure. First, customs did not allow transit containers, which account for between 30 and 37 percent of the total traffic, to leave the container terminal. Second, individual consignees had the right to designate a specific OCDY on the bill of lading.

4. The transfer of containers to a container freight station is done at a cost to the importer and is a concern.

5. The guarantee given to importers is that a CFS is not entitled to charge for storage after the importer has presented the customs release and requested to take possession of the container. The guarantee is used to limit this practice in Dar es Salaam, for instance. CFSs could also sabotage legitimate plans to increase port-handling capacity because they would lose market share.

6. In addition to the port storage tariff, shipping lines apply a container demurrage charge. This varies not only by line but also by consignee, with larger shippers receiving the most favorable rates. It is important to distinguish between port dues and port tariffs. Port dues are charges for general port services and facilities, whereas specific tariffs are for specific and clearly identified services (UNCTAD 1985). Cost-based pricing has been the traditional approach to pricing. A price is fixed on the basis of the costs incurred in providing the services or facilities. Three categories of costs are involved: fixed costs, which cannot be avoided whether or not the service or facility is used; variable cost of a service or facility, which is avoided if the service or facility is not used; and marginal cost of a service or facility, which is the extra cost incurred in providing a given service or facility for an additional time to the period originally intended. Variable and marginal costs take into consideration demand for port services and facilities. This is because these costs change in the short term and involve output, for instance, number of ships berthed, number of tons handled, and so forth (UNCTAD 1985). Key financial objectives of port management include (a) to be financially self-sufficient, (b) to earn a reasonable rate of return on assets, and (c) to provide adequate funds for investment in new facilities. Increasingly sophisticated organizational structure and increased demand for diverse functions have complicated the task of tariff formulation. Responsibility for tariff formulation has been transferred from the accounting department to standing committees or senior management, which then coordinates the inputs from various departments.

7. The free time for transit cargo is 21 days. The revised storage rates were initially US$12–US$14 per TEU per day.

8. Peter Masi, executive director, Dar es Salaam Corridor Committee.

9. The following section is extracted from Raballand and Mjekiqi (2010).

10. Section 31 (subsections 1–9) of the Nigerian customs regulation deals with "goods uncleared and missing goods" and recommends that the Board of Customs "may sell them" *without specific mention of any price*. Although there are guidelines, they appear to be subject to the discretionary powers of the comptroller general of customs, who exerts a delegated power on behalf of the chairman of the board (the minister of finance). These auction regulations apply only to overtime goods, not to seized goods.

11. SARS identified its top 20 clients for accreditation, which accords benefits such as green line, fewer inspections, and post-clearance audit, among others. These companies account for approximately 70–80 percent of total cargo.

12. Better relations with shipping companies have beneficial effects on reliability and responsiveness of ports (Song and Panayides 2008).

13. During the pilot stage, performance contracts were launched in two of the seven offices in the port of Douala that collect 76 percent of the port's

revenue. Office Douala Port I handles imports of goods in containers for home use, with the exception of vehicles, has 10 to 11 inspectors, and collects 60 percent of revenue. Office Douala Port V handles imports of vehicles, including in containers, has five to seven inspectors, and collects 16 percent of revenue. Like any other contract, the performance contracts formalize an agreement between two parties, specifying mutual obligations regarding results. The contracts went beyond revenue targets, which are fixed annually for the government by customs. For each objective, a comprehensive review was conducted to determine which parameters would be taken into account. Once these parameters were defined, the performance contract set a mini- mum or maximum threshold. This threshold is a median calculated on the basis of the declarations processed by the offices over the previous three years: 2007, 2008, and 2009. The sample covered 74,591 declarations for Office Douala Port I and 63,761 for Office Douala Port V.

14. The results compared the period under contracts from February to November 2010 to the same period in 2009. December and January were excluded because of seasonal concerns: economic activity increases during the Christmas period and so does the pressure on customs bureaus to achieve the annual revenue targets, which gives rise to specific procedures and low activity following Christmas.

15. The estimated revenue added during the pilot (all other things being equal) is equal to the revenues actually collected during the experiment minus the number of declarations during the experiment multiplied by the average taxes and duties of 2009.

16. In this regard, donors should disseminate a simple definition of dwell time from the time the container is discharged from a vessel to the time it is ready for collection by the importer.

References

Arnold, John. 1985. *Port Tariffs: Current Practices and Trends.* Washington, DC: World Bank.

Cantens, Thomas, Gaël Raballand, Samson Bilangna, and Djeuwo Marcellin. 2011. "Reforming Customs by Measuring Performance: A Cameroon Case Study." In *Where to Spend the Next Million? Applying Impact Evaluation to Trade Assistance*, ed. Olivier Cadot, Ana Fernandes, Julien Gourdon, and Aadiya Mattoo, 183–206. Washington, DC: World Bank.

Chetty, Mervin. 2011. "The Success Story of Durban." Presentation during the Tunis stakeholder workshop, December 13.

Raballand, Gaël, and Edmond Mjekiqi. 2010. "Nigeria's Trade Policy Facilitates Unofficial Trade but Not Manufacturing." In *Putting Nigeria to Work*, ed. Volker Treichel, 203–28 . Washington, DC: World Bank.

Song, Dong-Wook, and Photis M. Panayides. 2008. "Global Supply Chain and Port Terminals: Integration and Competitiveness." *Maritime Policy and Management* 35 (1): 73–87.

UNCTAD (United Nations Conference on Trade and Development). 1985. *Port Development: A Handbook for Planners in Developing Countries.* TD/B/C.4/175/ Rev. 1. New York: UNCTAD.

Detailed Information on the Case Studies

Operational Dwell Time

Mombasa

The port in Mombasa has 16 deepwater berths, five of which are used for container traffic. The equipment is only five to six years old, and reliability is high.[1] Average productivity at berth is 16–18 moves per vessel-hour, but this usually involves two cranes. Crane productivity is only 10–12 boxes per gross crane-hour and 12–13 per net crane-hour. This compares with more than 20 in modern ports. The low productivity is a result of congestion in the container yard as well as lack of reliable power. While equipment is reasonably reliable, the amount of equipment is not sufficient to meet peak demand. Two other berths, 13–14, have a length of 368 meters and alongside depth of 10.6 meters. These are dedicated to serving Maersk vessels, which are loaded and unloaded using their own gear. Kenya Ports Authority has equipped the adjoining storage area with three reachstackers. Maersk provides additional equipment in order to speed turnaround but is only able to achieve handling rates of 13 boxes per vessel-hour. Berths 13 and 14 have been handling an increasing portion of the port's container traffic.

The increase in the number of containers transferred per call, combined with the decline in average berth productivity due in part to the increase in the amount of containers handled at Berths 13–14, has increased the average time that vessels spend at berth to about three days to discharge about 900 boxes (1,200 20-foot equivalent units [TEUs]). Because of the limited amount of equipment, productivity is the same for larger vessels, which require five to six days to discharge 1,500 TEUs or more.

Occupancy for the container terminal has fluctuated between 80 and 90 percent for much of the last seven years. Severe congestion occurred in the middle of 2007 and again in 2008, when occupancy rose above 90 percent. Up through 2006, the average delay for vessels waiting for a berth was about 1.5 days, but by 2008, this figure was 2.5 days, even though the number of vessels waiting had decreased. In 2009, the average berth waiting time (for all vessels) decreased steadily as the number of vessels waiting declined. While waiting time is somewhat high for a modern port, it is low compared to that of other ports in the region.

Yard congestion is a continuing problem. In 2007, the container terminal had a backup area of about 12 hectares, with an additional 7.5 acres behind Berths 11–14. Together these provided a maximum design capacity of about 12,000 TEU and normal operating capacity of about 8,000 TEUs.[2] However, in early 2007, the confluence of peak winter traffic and lack of inland transport due to postelection violence led to yard occupancy of about 19,000 TEUs.

Tema

The Tema Container Terminal was constructed in 2002 on an existing timber pier located within the port's breakwater. The entrance channel restricts vessels to a maximum length of 246 meters and draft of 11.5 meters. The terminal has two berths. These have a length of 575 meters and can accommodate vessels with a draft of up to 11.5 meters. On the other side of the pier, Berths 3–5 are used for general cargo operations and can accommodate vessels with a draft up to 10 meters. In addition to the pier, the port has a main wharf with seven multipurpose berths, one of which is used to load and unload clinker. The terminal is equipped with three ship-to-shore gantry cranes (SSGs). Despite their age, they are able to achieve an average gross handling rate of 19–21 moves per hour.

Imports are stored in a separate area located to the west of the pier. One section is equipped with four old rubber-tired gantries (RTGs) used to block stack containers destined for the off-dock container yards (ODCYs). The rest of the yard has low-density stacking suitable for reachstacker operations. While a shortage of yard equipment has contributed to congestion in the past, efforts are under way to resolve this problem. Specifically, the number of RTGs is to be doubled.

The container terminal is operated by Meridian Port Services under a 20-year concession agreement.[3] As part of the agreement, the port transferred its container-handling equipment to the concession, and this accounts for a majority of the equipment in use. Under the agreement, Meridian Port Services was required to develop approximately 16.5 hectares of paved storage plus ancillary buildings. In return, it was given exclusive right to serve all vessels carrying more than 50 containers. In 2007, its market share was 85 percent. This decreased during the following year due to congestion, but has since recovered to more than 90 percent.

Vessel productivity is currently between 28 and 30 moves per hour at berth, but the net rate is much higher, because the time required for berthing, unberthing, and clearing the vessel often exceeds five hours. Most vessels can achieve turnaround in less than two days. The larger lines are able to achieve 35–40 moves per berth-hour, which allows a turnaround time of 1.5 days since the terminal operates 24 hours a day, seven days a week. Improvements in berth productivity have helped to moderate the increase in time at berth resulting from the increase in the amount of containers transferred per vessel call. However, the increase in waiting time for a berth has led to an increase in overall port turnaround time.

Berth waiting time peaked at the end of 2008 because of heightened security measures during the period of national elections and subsequent change in procedures with the new government. This coincided with the annual peak in traffic prior to Christmas and Chinese New Year. At one point, the delays reached 20 days. Prior to that, significant delays in 2007 were due to the combination of low berth productivity preceding handover of terminal operations to Meridian Port Services and construction of the new storage area. While exceptional circumstances caused the delays in both years, there was also a cyclical problem caused by seasonal peaks in demand, especially at the end of the year. The problem reoccurred at the end of 2009, when the annual surge caused congestion in the storage areas, with the result that not only the terminal but also all of the ODCYs were full and dwell times increased significantly.

Dar es Salaam
Tanzania International Container Terminal has a design water depth of 12.2 meters, but the actual depth is less than 10.5 meters because of

siltation. The length of the ships is limited to 234 meters as a result of a bend in the one-way approach channel. This presents a problem for bulk vessels, but not for container vessels, which currently average 160 meters. The 749-meter wharf can accommodate three vessels but lacks a backup area to serve this many vessels efficiently. The original area of 18 hectares has been increased to about 23 hectares. The 12-hectare storage yard used to have ground slots of 2,500 TEUs, but now has 3,860 TEUs. Additional container storage has been added outside the terminal, both within the port and outside in the off-dock yards and empty container depots.

Berth productivity increased dramatically at the start of the concession but has since declined due to unreliable equipment and congestion in the terminal yard.[4] Two of the three ship-to-shore gantry cranes are more than 20 years old. Four of the 12 RTGs are about 20 years old, and the rest are about 10 years old. While seven RTGs have been added since 2007, the number of available SSGs declined during 2008–09, when one was out of commission for most of the year. Eventually, two mobile container cranes were brought in, but these had low productivity.

In 2009, the productivity of the two working SSGs was 19.6 moves per net working hour. This is reasonable given the age of the equipment. When nonproductive periods are included, this drops to 17.1 moves per gross crane-hour. The high level of berth occupancy has meant that most vessels use only one SSG, with the result that vessel productivity is similar to crane productivity. However, during the last two years, the loss of one SSG combined with yard congestion caused vessel productivity to decline to an average of 14.5 moves per net ship-hour.

The increase in the amount of containers transferred per call and the decline in berth productivity meant that vessel turnaround time increased. Occupancy increases because space must be reserved for the containers that are being unloaded and loaded. While unloading time had relatively little impact on dwell time up until 2007, since then, it has added more than a day to average dwell time. For the largest vessels, with turnaround times of four to five days, it has added more than two days.

Because neither the length of the wharf nor berth productivity increased with traffic, there was a dramatic increase in berth occupancy beginning in 2005. As berth occupancy rose above 80 percent, congestion at berth accelerated, and vessel waiting time increased sharply.

The nominal capacity of the yard in the container terminal was about 9,000 TEUs up until 2009, based on an average stacking height of three.

Occupancy approached 100 percent of nominal capacity in 2007 and reached 150 percent in 2008, creating severe congestion in the yard. This made it difficult to keep track of containers and to manage yard inventory, which increased average dwell time and the level of congestion. In order to address this problem, the storage area was expanded, and nominal capacity rose to about 15,000 TEUs, including the areas behind Berths 1 and 7. In addition, a network of off-dock container yards was introduced.

Lomé

Container ships are operated on a 250-meter-long, two-berth pier by two private terminal operating companies, SE2M and Manuport, but so far, there is no container terminal configuration as such. Regular calls are composed of both mother ships for east-west routes and feeder vessels for the region. Five mobile quay cranes in good condition are used for container transfers, with a satisfactory productivity at berth of 18 to 20 movements per hour. Other ports in the region have higher productivity, but Lomé needs to move to a proper container terminal configuration for operational performance to improve. Most vessel turnaround is about two days, but some congestion at berth has been evident recently, with up to 30 hours delay at buoy. Container traffic has increased four to fivefold since stevedoring activities were privatized in 2001; as a consequence, the port has reached the upper limit of its container-handling capacity. Two major projects are under way to expand capacity: the construction of a new pier dedicated to container traffic and the construction of a new port with capacity of 1.5 million TEUs. With its natural advantages and free port status, the port of Lomé attracts important transshipment flows, and shipping lines are willing to invest in its strategic potential.

Container storage areas consist of a series of platforms operated by SE2M and Manuport that cover about 20 hectares in total for a storage capacity of about 10,000 containers. New platforms are being built to meet growing demand. A dedicated container freight station enables shippers to break bulk cargo within the port, and most containers are emptied there. The port is operated in a low-density four-level reach-stacker configuration with modern yard equipment. Together with the modernization of infrastructure and superstructure, Manuport and SE2M have invested in modern terminal operating systems, and operational performance is no longer a bottleneck in the clearance process.

Douala

In the port of Douala, berth congestion is due to a shortage of capacity, given average berth occupancy of 60 percent. Net crane productivity could be improved through better maintenance of the two gantry cranes, which have not yet reached half of their lifetime. The investment in a third gantry crane is not yet economically justified, but it will be if traffic increases. Efficient dredging could improve berth productivity by extending the availability of berths.

As for yard productivity, the main issue today is the very high occupancy rate (88 percent). Physical extension of yard area would be difficult given the shortage of available land in the port outskirts and would require either additional movements or much longer distances between the peers and storage places. The pavement of a small area in the import yard is expected to increase yard capacity by a few hundred TEUs, and the transfer of very long-stay containers and confiscated containers to a separate storage area could also release some capacity. A substantial increase in capacity is, however, only achievable through investment in a more intensive storage configuration and a transfer from the current reachstacker configuration to a straddle carrier configuration (capacity increase of 40 to 50 percent). See figure A.1 for operational dwell time in Douala port.

Durban

The Durban Container Terminal has benefited substantially from major infrastructure investments, and it now comprises a new terminal known as Pier 1 and the old terminal known as Pier 2. With a capacity of 720,000 TEUs, Pier 1 has three berths with an 11.9-meter draft, six SSG_S with 888 reefer points, and RTGs. Pier 2 is designed for a capacity of 2.9 million TEUs, and it boasts six berths over 14,000 ground slots, with an average draft of 11.8 meters, 19 ship-to-shore gantries, and 1,117 reefer points.[5]

Figure A.1   Operational Dwell Time in Douala Port

| operational dwell time | vessel arrival at buoy | vessel berthing & container discharge 24h to 48h | transfer to the yard or ODCY <1h | delivery onto truck <2h | exit from yard 1h to 8h |

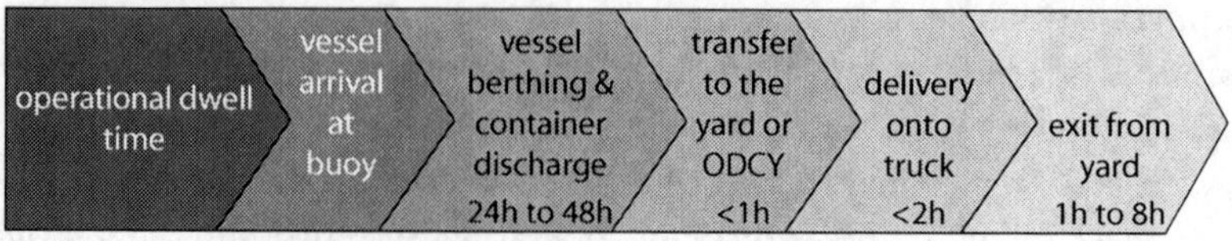

Source: Authors, based on data from Douala International Terminal.
Note: h = hour.

Transactional Dwell Time

Mombasa

Kenya Revenue Authority, which generates 95 percent of government funding, obtains 40 percent of its revenue from duties and value added taxes collected by the Customs Services Department. As a result, considerable attention is given to maximizing this revenue, including setting revenue targets for individual customs offices, conducting extensive reviews of customs declarations, and undertaking high rates of physical inspection.

Kenya Revenue Authority does not employ a destination inspection service. The local shipping agencies file their vessel manifests at least two days prior to the arrival of the vessel. The carrying and forwarding (C&F) agents file their customs declaration after the manifest has been registered with customs. These are filed electronically using the Simba system, which Kenya Revenue Authority introduced in 2005. The system is designed to handle scanned copies of the supporting documents, but this has not been implemented, with the exception of government documents.[6]

After the declaration has been lodged with customs, the consignee pays the duties and taxes computed by the Simba system based on the self-assessment. Once the payment has been made, the C&F agent delivers a folder with the declaration and supporting documents to the declaration validation point, where they are reviewed and a final decision is made regarding the level of inspection. Once a customs release has been issued, the C&F agent pays the port charges and outstanding shipping charges and the delivery order is issued, allowing the container to exit the port.

The level of inspection—green, yellow, amber, red channel—is determined once the declaration has been lodged. Currently, nearly all import containers are subject to physical inspection, but this varies from a brief visual check to removal and inspection of all of the contents of the container. For shipments of homogeneous goods in multiple containers, only one container is usually inspected. The average time to clear an import container at the Mombasa container terminal is three days. For green channel inspections, the time is two days or less, for the red channel, it is three to four days. This time refers only to the period from lodging to assignment of a level of inspection in addition to a period from presentation of the folder to the customs office and issuance of the customs release.

There are fewer procedures for clearing transit containers than for clearing imports. The C&F agent submits the transit declaration with supporting documents, including bill of lading, invoice, and packing list. The customs officer checks that seals are intact and occasionally performs a physical inspection. The container generally can be released within a day, provided that the C&F agent has paid the port fees and arranged for inland transport. Inland transport can introduce delays since the container must be transported under a bond provided by the C&F agent or importer. This procedure should require one day if the C&F agent has a sufficient bond.[7]

Some of the additional dwell time can be explained by the additional scrutiny given to commodities such as sugar and automobiles that have a high risk of diversion because duties are high. However, constraints on landside transport explain part of the problem. Deterioration in the availability of rail service has reduced the amount of transit boxes moved by rail to 6 percent. The increase in demand for bonded transport has created delays in obtaining vehicles. In addition, delays en route for trucks carrying transit cargo have effectively reduced fleet capacity.

Tema

Ghana's clearance procedures for import and inbound transit cargo are unnecessarily complex and redundant. However, delays are avoided by allowing the clearance process to begin up to three weeks prior to the arrival of cargo. Processing time is reduced through the use of electronic exchange of documents using a common platform, GCNet. This platform links shipping lines, C&F agents, customs officials, and other supply chain participants. As a result, the amount of container dwell time attributable to clearance procedures is generally four days or less.

Ghana currently employs a destination inspection scheme (DIS) to review the initial declarations form prior to arrival of the container in port. The import declaration form (IDF) is submitted to the DIS prior to arrival of the cargo, together with a pro forma invoice, supplementary information document, and tax identification number. Since 2009, the IDF can be submitted electronically, which significantly reduces the time for processing. By early 2010, about half were filed in this manner. The DIS reviews the documents for correctness of the classification and valuation. The latter involves contacting a network of DIS agents operating outside of the country, a process usually requiring three to 10 days. Once approved and after the final invoice, bill of lading, and packing list have been submitted, a final classification and valuation report (FCVR) is issued.

Following electronic transmission of the FCVR, the C&F agent submits to customs the hard copy together with the customs declaration and supporting documents. The documents are then checked by customs, the Ghana Shippers Council, and the Ministry of Trade and Industry, and the import declaration is lodged in customs' computer system. For containers that are to be scanned or physically inspected, the C&F agent makes an appointment with customs. For scanning, the container is moved to the scanner facility adjoining the container terminal. For physical inspection, it is moved to the Shed 10 area for containers in the port and to a dedicated inspection facility for containers in the ODCY.

Once the inspection has been completed, customs issues a release order and the cargo can exit the port or ODCY. At the gate, the Ghana Ports and Harbours Authority (GPHA) security personnel verify the declaration against the cargo loaded onto the truck and also verify that the required GPHA charges have been paid; then Ghana customs and other security agencies conduct a final examination before releasing the vehicle.

The high rate of scanning and physical inspection is intended to discourage misrepresentation rather than to increase collections. A sample of customs records indicates that additional charges and fines collected as a result of inspection represent less than 1 percent of total collections. Efforts to increase the proportion of shipments assigned green channel status focus on the Customs Gold Card Program. Currently, about 144 large companies are in the program, mostly multinationals. These shippers receive multiple-container shipments but represent less than 20 percent of total shipments. Despite its success, the program has not been expanded. Moreover, customs opens the green channel for containers as they leave the port for a visual check.

The amber and red channel designations increase the clearance time by one to three days. The typical time from lodgment to release is three to five days for the red channel versus about three days for the yellow channel. Both require moving containers from the stacks to the designated inspection area. The physical inspection requires more time to organize, but the scanning requires waiting in a queue for the scanner. Containers in the port that are subject to physical inspection must exit the container terminal and pay all handling charges before being delivered to a shed for inspection.

Dar es Salaam

Pre-clearance can begin prior to receipt of the vessel manifest. The Tanzania Inspection Service Company (TISCAN) can issue a preliminary classification and valuation report prior to receipt of scanned copies of the final bill of lading, actual invoice, and certificate of origin. After receiving these documents, it issues the final classification and valuation report. The FCVR is sent to customs in electronic format for entering the customs declaration in the ASYCUDA (Automated System for Customs Data). Once the vessel manifest has been received, a release order is issued. In 2009, about 97 percent of the IDFs were lodged at the time of arrival of the cargo versus only 30 percent in 2007. However, only about 85 percent of the FCVRs were issued prior to arrival of the cargo.

The results from a 2009 time release study indicate an average of 19 days to complete pre-clearance from submission by the C&F agent of the IDF application to receipt of the FCVR. TISCAN accounts for about 5.5 days, while the C&F agent accounts for 13.5 days. The former includes not only the time for processing but also the time between initial application and submission of the final IDF. Most of the latter is the time between submission of the final version of the IDF and submission of the final supporting documents.

The time required to unload the vessel and place the container in the stack is, on average, one day. The mean time from arrival to lodgment of the customs declaration is about six days, with a standard error of 180 percent. The time from lodgment to issuance of the customs release order is seven days, with a standard error of 85 percent. A further 3.5 days, on average, are required to complete formalities, arrange for transport, and remove the container from the terminal. The average of seven days between lodging the customs declaration and receiving the customs release order includes one day for confirmation of payment, one day for the C&F agent to submit the file for clearance after being assigned a clearance channel, and two days for customs to complete inspection and issue the customs release order.

In 2008, the clearance process for cargo assigned to the green channel averaged about 14 days, whereas cargo assigned to scanning averaged almost 15.7 days and cargo requiring physical inspection required an additional 0.25 day, on average. For goods that are subject to processing by other government agencies, the additional time required for clearance was about 1.5 days, on average. For import containers transferred to off-dock yards, the total time in port averaged about 18 days, of which 6.5 were required to move cargo from the vessel to the stacks in the ODCY. This time was considerably reduced in 2010.

A major contributor to the relatively long average storage time is long-stay cargo. Typically, this is government or project cargo waiting for tax-exemption certification or cargo for which the consignee does not have the necessary funds to pay for its release. Under customs regulation, this is classified as long-stay cargo after 21 days. It is then subject to auction by customs; however, the procedure for notifying the consignee and preparing auction generally requires one to two months. Because of the difficulty of conducting a transparent audit, customs is reluctant to perform this function. However, in response to the growing problem of long-stay cargo, customs has begun to perform regular auctions.

Lomé

The customs clearance process has been reformed with the introduction of ASYCUDA++. However, redundancies between the former paperwork process and the current electronic system cause long clearance delays. The main sequence of customs clearance formalities is composed of the following documentary steps:

- Registration of the ship manifest by the consignee on ASYCUDA++ after vessel arrival
- Cargo delivery bill (*bon à délivrer*) handed over by the consignee to the shipper during exchange of the bill of lading
- Cargo clearance bill (*bon à enlever*) given by customs after receipt of the customs declaration and the payment of fees
- Cargo exit bill (*bon de sortie*) given by the port authority after the payment of port fees (valid for three days)
- Bill reissued by the Port Operations Department to confirm the payment of fees and register the exit date
- Delivery note issued by the Port Operations Department to confirm in writing the exit from port or transfer to a container freight station
- Order of execution issued by the Customs Brigade to confirm and verify liquidation of the customs declaration

Additional steps are sometimes necessary (for example, exemptions or special authorizations); as a consequence, clearance often exceeds 20 days.

Douala

In Douala, the layout of the port platform is ill adapted to the physical role of a container terminal (transfer area), and the creation of an independent customs area dedicated to physical or scanning inspections is being discussed (see figure A.2). The Comité National de Facilitation du Trafic Maritime International advocates the performance of physical

Figure A.2   Transactional Dwell Time in Douala Port

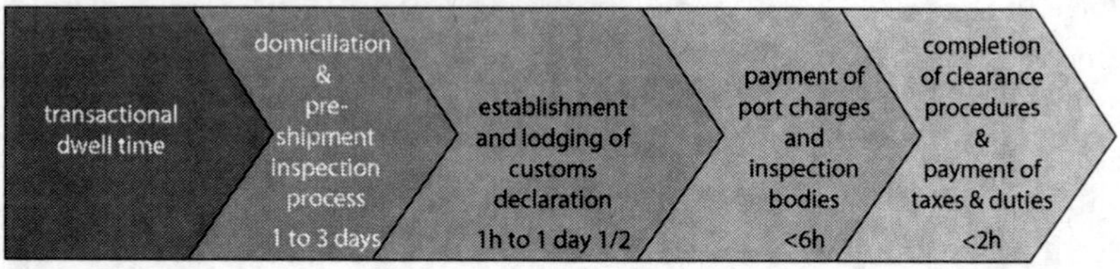

| transactional dwell time | domiciliation & pre-shipment inspection process 1 to 3 days | establishment and lodging of customs declaration 1h to 1 day 1/2 | payment of port charges and inspection bodies <6h | completion of clearance procedures & payment of taxes & duties <2h |

Source: Authors based on data from GUCE
Note: h = hour.

inspections of the truck to avoid double rehandling, but this would probably immobilize trucks to the detriment of trucking companies. Obstacles to an efficient gate exit also include poor connectivity of the customs booth and redundancy in document controls after the release has been issued.

Trade facilitation has been at the forefront of trade policy in Cameroon for almost 10 years, with initiatives and investments aimed at increasing trade performance by improving transport infrastructure, removing corruption and informal practices, modernizing customs administration, reducing nontariff trade barriers, improving revenue collection and border controls, and reducing transaction and administrative costs. A multidonor transit and transport facilitation project is being co-financed by the World Bank, the African Development Bank, and the European Commission to help Cameroon, the Central African Republic, and Chad to address these challenges. Much has been achieved in the course of the last 10 years. The modernization of customs administration and the introduction of a one-stop shop for clearance procedures (the Guichet Unique du Commerce Extérieur [GUCE]) have led to an estimated savings of more than 11 days in average clearance time (figure A.3).

A threshold of three days seems to be a lower limit for time-efficiency of manual procedures, and the GUCE is aiming to dematerialize procedures (to make them paperless) to achieve better performance. In parallel, the customs administration has recently introduced performance contracts to ensure better efficiency of customs operations in the port, and one indicator (time release) tracks the time period in between the broker's registration and the customs officer's assessment. The percentage of declarations assessed the day they are lodged has increased from 70 to 90 percent.

Customs clearance does not seem to be a priority for efforts to reduce dwell time in Douala. Of course, there is still room for improvement, in

Figure A.3   Time Necessary to Perform Customs Clearance Formalities in Douala Port, 2000–09

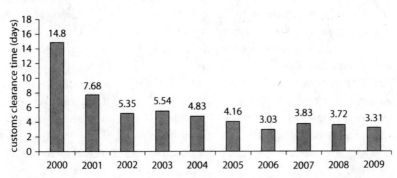

Source: GUCE 2010.

particular, in the preshipment inspection process and lodging of the customs declaration.

Durban

The target for the South African Revenue Services (SARS) is to clear within three hours declarations processed through Electronic Data Interchange (EDI). According to SARS, during the first quarter of 2011, the average time to release goods was three hours when processed through EDI (75 percent of declarations) and 10 hours when not processed through EDI.

With customs clearing cargo in less than one day and Transnet Ports Authority moving cargo efficiently from the terminal area, it is safe to assume that there is no "transactional dwell time" at the port of Durban, according to one stakeholder (or at least it is rather limited by the standards of Southern Africa or Sub-Saharan Africa).

The customs modernization project made a significant contribution to improving the competitiveness of the port of Durban. The project delivery strategy of enhanced compliance recognized three key elements influencing customs operations: (a) some taxpayers or traders will always try to comply whether enforcement is effective or not, (b) the undecided majority will choose one way or the other based on how well the strategy is implemented, and (c) some taxpayers or traders—criminals—will not comply whether enforcement is effective or not.

Within that context, the strategy sought to improve services, making it easy for those who want to comply, and to improve enforcement, making it hard for those who do not want to comply. Therefore, measures were initiated to increase treatment differentiation and compliance.

In this regard, contractualization between customs brokers and customs was developed. For instance, companies wishing to be authorized as an economic operator need to go through detailed interviews and be transparent regarding their economic activities and supply operations; from time to time, they are inspected randomly. However, these companies benefit from a green channel, which means that, cargo can be removed as soon as it is handled at the port.[8] Contrary to most countries in Sub-Saharan Africa, pre-clearance is the rule, and this explains why the target for customs clearance is in hours and not in days, as in other countries.

Notes

1. Because Kenya Ports Authority lacks sufficient yard tractors and trailers, the shipping lines provide supplementary equipment.

2. Berth throughput begins to decline as yard occupancy rises above 8,000 TEUs.

3. A corporation whose largest shareholder is Bolloré and that includes A. P. Møeller as a major shareholder. This effectively gives the two major lines a presence on the board.

4. The concession of the container terminal did not produce a significant increase in net handling rates but did reduce the proportion of delay time from 28 percent of net working time in 2001 to 8 percent in 2005, which, in effect, resulted in a 30 percent increase in productivity. Since then, delay time has risen sharply, reaching 23 percent in 2007.

5. The port operates 24 hours a day and 365 days a year. During daylight hours, the ships are restricted to 243.8-meter length with a maximum width of 35 meters and a draft of 11.9 meters or 12.2 meters according to tide and harbor master service. The largest ship calling in 2009 had a 6,742-TEU carrying capacity, which is relatively small by world standards but probably the largest to call at any African port.

6. Orbus software is intended to transmit scans of documents produced by government agencies, including prearrival documents from government agencies and pro forma invoices.

7. However, the dwell time for containers averages 11 days due in part to delays in organizing inland movement and in part to the decision to take advantage of the free time period.

8. SARS identified its top 20 clients to get accreditation, with benefits such as green line designation, fewer inspections, and post-clearance audit. These companies account for approximately 70–80 percent of total cargo.

Reference

GUCE (Guichet Unique du Commerce Extérieur). 2010. "Synthèse sur les délais de passage portuaire." Direction Générale des Études et Pilotage de la Performance, September.

A Simplified Analytical Demand Model of Container Dwell Times in Port

This appendix describes the economic foundations of rational decisions with regard to container storage in port terminals and off-dock container yards (ODCYs).

Storage operations can be defined as a subcomponent of an international logistics pathway that starts with loading containers in the supplier's facilities and ends with unloading them in the customer's facilities. We define logistics pathway as "a sequential set of logistics operations, warehousing, depot operations, port operations, trucking, and freight forwarding, which deal with the end-to-end movement of freight" (Magala and Sammons 2008). In addition, we focus on containerized trade only, specifically containerized trade through international ports.

When deciding to import a certain quantity of containerized cargo, shippers have to choose either directly or indirectly (through contracted shipping and freight forwarding agents or logistics providers) what logistics pathway to use. This is an informed supply chain decision that is generally based on a combination of rational criteria such as cost, delivery time, frequency, and risk as well as some behavioral patterns (for example, repeat-buyer behaviors).

Our objective is to model how shippers make rational decisions about logistics pathways and, more specifically, what are the drivers of demand for storage in port terminals or ODCYs. Figure B.1 presents the set of players involved.

By adopting a demand approach, we assume here that importers are the leading decision makers in the selection of the logistics pathway and that they rationally select a logistics pathway based on maximization of their utility.

We construct our demand model by adopting an abstract mode—an abstract commodity—approach that describes freight and storage alternatives by a vector of attributes rather than physical reality (Quandt and Baumol 1969). Likewise, commodities are defined by a set of characteristics such as unit price or packaging and not by the commodity itself.

In the abstract mode approach, two shipping alternatives that share the same attributes relevant to shippers (for example, transit time, cost, level of service) are considered equal. And shippers arguably do not distinguish between two such shipping options because they are generally chosen by carrying and forwarding (C&F) agents and shipping lines with little information along the maritime transport route (for example, survey results confirm shippers have little information about the transshipment hub used for their cargo).

A shipping alternative is therefore specified as a vector $X_i = X_{i1}, X_{i2} \ldots X_{in}$, where the element X_{ij} is the value of the jth variable (for example, daily storage cost) characterizing shipping alternative i. Likewise, two commodities that share common characteristics (density of value, packaging) can be considered identical from a logistics viewpoint and are referred to using an equivalent vector $Y = Y_{i1}, Y_{i2} \ldots Y_{im}$.

Figure B.1   Demand System for Container Imports

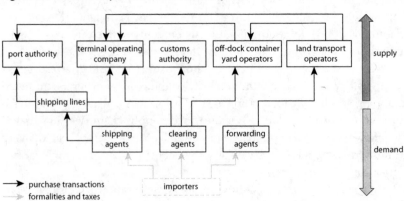

Source: Authors.

We start by formulating total logistics costs associated with the selection of a logistics pathway and then construct a deterministic decision-making model based on minimization of these total logistics costs. Next, we look at profits rather than costs and at how profit maximization strategies translate into the selection of a logistics pathway. Then we extend the analysis to a nondeterministic context in which model inputs cannot be precisely estimated ex ante. The nondeterministic model is especially attractive for its ability to explain non-optimality. We finish by offering some concluding remarks and relax, in particular, the assumption of perfect rationality.

Cost Minimization

Total Logistics Cost Formulation in a Scenario of Perfect Certainty

The logistics pathway depicted in figure B.2 for an international container trade operation consists of the sequence of an export and an import operation. The exporter (supplier) and the importer (customer) are both referred to as "shippers" because they are involved in selecting an international shipping alternative. A large set of international commercial terms (Incoterms) define precisely what is the responsibility of each player. Without loss of generality, we can assume that the typical split of responsibilities is as shown in figure B.2, with some variation for operations in the dotted boxes.

Figure B.2   Typical Sequence of Operations under the Responsibility of Exporters and Importers for International Container Trade

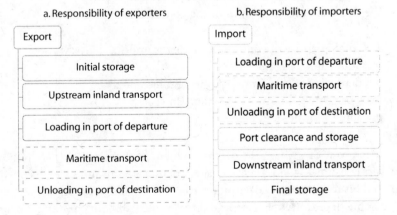

Source: Authors.

In this section, we formulate total logistics costs (TLCs) for a standard import operation and model the choice of a logistics pathway by importers as the deterministic output of the minimization of this TLC. We therefore focus only on the sequence of operations described in figure B.2, panel b.

We start by defining a fixed container handling cost, r_h, that encompasses both loading operations in the port of departure and unloading in the port of destination (terminal handling charges, transfer cost).

Maritime transport is defined by two variables: (a) a shipping rate, r_m, and (b) maritime transit time, t_m. The port clearance and storage leg comprises all fees and procedures attached to port clearance and storage in a port or an off-dock container yard before loading on a truck or train for final transport to the customer's facility. Let us define u_p as the variable port clearance cost (mainly storage cost, per storage day). Imported containers transiting through a given port of destination generally spend a number of days, t_p, in this port or its dependencies (ODCYs) that is the sum of three components:

t_1 = transfer time (to unload the container from the vessel and transfer it to the yard)

t_2 = storage time spent in the container terminal or ODCY before loading it onto a truck or train

t_3 = procedural time (for clearance procedures and controls).

t_1 is a port attribute that we assume is identical for all shippers and is insignificant with respect to t_2 and t_3,[1] while t_2 and t_3 are specific attributes depending on both the commodity and the shipper.

We also use other attributes of the commodities:

T = total quantity of commodity Y that is imported yearly
V = unit value of commodity Y
b = depreciation rate (interest plus obsolescence)
s = mean interval between reorders (in years)
r_d = rate for duties and taxes.

Whatever the final use of the commodity imported (production input, consumer goods), we consider here that the importer has estimated his total quantity of imports T for the ongoing year and has opted for some fixed-interval fixed-quantity replenishment strategy. Other replenishment strategies can be considered later as derived from this simplified case.

We then define the following:

a = cost of ordering and processing a new reorder
d = discount rate
i_p = average inventory level in the port or ODCY storage facility
i_f = average inventory level in the private storage facility.

Inland transport is defined by freight rate, r_i, and freight transit time, t_i. Final storage is available at variable cost u_f, with storage time t_f.

Let us then formulate the total logistics cost of our shipper with regard to imports of commodity Y in the ongoing year:

$$\text{TLC} = \text{ordering cost} + \text{maritime shipping costs} +$$
$$\text{port clearance cost} + \text{inland transport cost} +$$
$$\text{final storage cost} + \text{financial cost.} \qquad \text{(B.1)}$$

We consider these six terms one at a time:

1. Ordering cost = cost per reorder × number of reorders = a/s
2. Maritime shipping cost = shipping rate × total quantity shipped = $r_m T$
3. Port clearance cost = fixed clearance cost + variable clearance cost, where fixed clearance cost = fixed container handling cost × amount shipped = $r_h T$ and variable clearance cost = cost per unit of time × storage time × inventory level = $u_p t_p i_p$
4. Inland transport cost = freight rate × total quantity shipped = $r_i T$
5. Final storage cost = cost per unit of time × storage time × inventory level = $u_f t_f i_f$
6. Financial cost = taxes + depreciation + cost of capital, where taxes = rate for taxes and duties × unit value × amount shipped = $r_d VT$, depreciation cost = depreciation rate × unit value × amount shipped × total transit time = $bVT (t_m + t_p + t_i + t_f)$, and cost of capital = discount rate × total early payment × coverage time.

Early payment consists of the payment of all taxes, duties, charges, and fees to agents in charge of shipping and clearance operations as soon as cargo exits the port. Coverage time is time between this payment and the effective sale and is thus equal to t_f. We therefore have the following:

$$\text{Cost of capital} = dt_f (r_m T + r_h T + u_p t_p i_p + r_i T + r_d VT). \qquad \text{(B.2)}$$

We now combine the six elements of the cost function (functions 1–6) to obtain:

$$TLC = \frac{a}{s} + (1 + dt_f)\,(r_m T + r_h T + u_p t_p i_p + r_i T + r_d VT) +$$
$$u_f t_f i_f + bVT\,(t_m + t_p + t_i + t_f). \qquad (B.3)$$

Cost Minimization in a Scenario of Perfect Certainty

In function B.3, there are seven alternative variables for shipping, r_m, r_h, t_1, t_m, t_i, u_p, and u_f, and nine commodity- or shipper-specific variables, a, s, T, t_2, t_3, t_f, r_d, r_i, and V. The two inventory-level variables, i_p and i_f, are a function of transit time and order quantity.

We now consider different situations that confront shippers, depending on the storage facilities available before final delivery. From a logistical point of view, shippers can be split into two limit cases: shippers who use their private facilities or third-party storage facilities outside the port as their main warehouse and shippers who use the storage services of the port and its dependencies as their primary warehouse.[2] This segmentation is a critical dimension of logistics chains in Africa when it comes to port dwell time in container terminals, and it goes back to the differentiation between "bottleneck-derived terminalization," in which the port terminal is essentially a source of delay and a capacity constraint in the shippers' supply chains, and "warehousing-derived terminalization," in which the terminal replaces warehousing facilities of the shippers and gradually becomes a strategic storage unit (Rodrigue and Notteboom 2009). We show here that this "warehousing-derived terminalization," together with the cost minimization and profit maximization strategies of shippers, is the main explanation for long dwell times in African ports.

Shippers without private storage facilities. We start by looking at the cost minimization behavior of shippers who do not have private storage facilities and who have to leave their cargo in the port storage area until final delivery to clients or production facilities. For those shippers, we have

$$i_f = 0 \text{ and } t_f = 0. \qquad (B.4)$$

The only inventory hold is therefore i_p (inventory in port or ODCY), and in a scenario of perfect certainty average inventory level is

$$i_p = \frac{Ts}{2}. \qquad (B.5)$$

Equation B.3 therefore becomes

$$TLC = \frac{a}{s} + T\left[r_m + r_h + \frac{1}{2} + u_p t_p s + r_i + r_d V + bV\left(t_m + t_p + t_i + t_f\right)\right].$$ (B.6)

Total logistics cost is therefore strictly growing with respect to all time markers t_m, t_p, and t_i, and a rational cost-minimization behavior would therefore lead shippers to minimize transit and dwell times.

Shippers now must determine the optimal replenishment interval, s. Cost minimization with respect to s leads to

$$\frac{\partial TLC}{\partial s} = \frac{-a}{s^2} + \frac{u_p t_p T}{2} = 0,$$ (B.7)

so that

$$s = \sqrt{\frac{2a}{u_p t_p T}}.$$ (B.8)

For example, if we set

Cost per reorder, a = US$400 per TEU (20-foot equivalent unit)
Port storage cost, u_p = two weeks free time, u_p = US$20 per day for the next two weeks, and u_p = US$40 per day thereafter
t_p = 25 days
Annual quantity imported, T = 200 TEUs,

the optimal interval time s would be equal to 52 days, and there would be seven reorders per year.

The optimized interval between reorders is inversely proportionate to t_p, which is the time to perform all physical operations, controls, and procedures in the port. An inefficient port clearance system with very long clearance time would therefore encourage shippers to have shorter replenishment intervals and split their annual orders into smaller and more frequent delivery batches.

Shippers with private storage facilities. Let us now consider shippers who possess or have access to some storage facilities outside the port. Assumption B.4 is no longer valid.

As soon as clearance procedures and controls are completed, shippers choose between the two storage options: leaving cargo inside the container terminal or ODCY and clearing it and storing it in their own storage facilities. Let us analyze these two options:

$$\Delta TLC = \frac{1}{2} Ts\,\tau\,(u_f - u_p) + T\tau^2 d\,(r_m + r_h + r_i + r_d V),$$ (B.9)

where τ is the additional number of days that the cargo would have to stay in the port in the first option.

The condition for this difference to be negative is therefore

$$\Delta TLC < 0 <=> u_f < u_p - \frac{2d}{s}\left(r_m + r_h + r_i + r_dV\right). \qquad \text{(B.10)}$$

In other words, if the extra financial cost subsequent to an early clearance of cargo from the port outweighs the potential savings in storage cost, there is no benefit to clearing the cargo from the expensive port storage area and moving it to cheaper storage facilities outside the port.

Despite potential savings in inventory holding costs, shippers might therefore be willing to leave their cargo in the container terminal or ODCY because they cannot pay all of the port clearance charges and fees in advance. Instead, they wait until they have sold the cargo to pay these expenses.

For example, if we set the unit cost per TEU as follows:

Port storage cost, u_p = two weeks free time; u_p = US$20 a day for the next two weeks; u_p = US$40 a day thereafter
Private storage cost, u_f = US$15 a day
Shipping rate, r_m = US$1,200
Container handling charge, r_h = US$300
Freight rate, r_i = US$75
Rate for taxes and duties, r_d = 20 percent
Discount rate = 12 percent per year (0.032 percent per day)
Interval between orders, s = 1/4 (one order every three months)
Cargo value, V = US$20,000 per TEU,

we get $2d/s\left(r_m + r_h + r_i + r_dV\right)$ = US$15, and condition B.10 would therefore happen only after four weeks. In this scenario, the shipper would leave the container in the port for a full month even if cargo were cleared more quickly.

In reality, we get a very important justification for long dwell times: clearance is cash-eager.

In our example, the shipper would have to pay US$5,575 in advance to clear his or her cargo from port, which is a significant amount of money that he might not have in hand before concluding the sale. The financial cost for early clearance (US$15 per TEU) is valued more heavily if the shipper faces cash constraints, as is often the case with imports of commodity products or with new producers, and clearance from port would be even more delayed in such a case. As we see later, many importers eventually abandon their cargo in the port because they cannot afford these advance payments.

From Cost Minimization to Profit Maximization

Our analysis so far has assumed that shippers take logistical decisions by trying to minimize total logistics costs. This is a rational, though partially inaccurate, assumption. It is more accurate to state that shippers take logistical decisions by trying to optimize profits. Now the reality is that, in a perfectly competitive market, prices are exogenous, and the final price of commodity Y is therefore independent from the logistical decisions of individual shippers. Because profits equal revenues minus costs, optimizing profits equals minimizing costs in these situations.

But if we assume that the price of commodity Y is affected by the logistical decisions of shippers, we have a different situation. Let us use π to define profits and R to define revenues. We have revenues equal unit price times total sales:

$$R = pT, \tag{B.11}$$

where p is the unit price of commodity Y.

The price of commodity Y can be affected at different levels by market conditions and the logistical decisions of shippers. Let us analyze an alternative pricing scenario before coming to any conclusions about the potential outputs of profit maximization strategies.

Pricing Strategies of Monopolists

We begin by analyzing which alternative pricing strategies a monopolist can adopt. Monopolies are very particular situations, in which a single firm accounts for the total sales of a given product Y. In such a context, this firm can arbitrarily set the price p of product Y, and customers will have no choice but to purchase the product at that price or to refuse to purchase it.

A monopolistic position is advantageous because the firm has very strong market power. However, the profit that this firm would make in alternative pricing scenarios also depends on market demand, and despite its power to set the price p at any desired level, the firm cannot force customers to purchase the product.

If we have a smooth demand function D as in figure B.3, for any given annual level of output T_e, we can demonstrate that there is a unique

Figure B.3   Monopoly Equilibrium

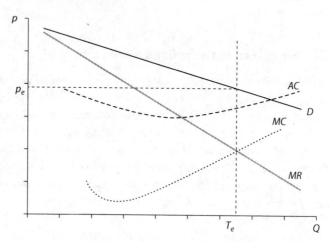

Source: Authors.
Note: AC = average cost; D = demand; MC = marginal cost; MR = marginal revenue; p = price; p_e = optimal price; T_e = annual level of output; Q = output.

optimal price p_e that would optimize profits of the monopolist firm. This price is the unique solution of the following equation:

$$\frac{\partial \pi}{\partial T} = 0 \lessgtr \frac{\partial R}{\partial T} - \frac{\partial TLC}{\partial T} = 0, \qquad (B.12)$$

which we can also write as $MR = MC$, where MR is the marginal revenue $\partial R/\partial T$ and MC is the marginal cost $\partial TLC/\partial T$.

In this case, the optimal price p_e is higher than the equilibrium price that would be observed in a competitive market and the corresponding annual level of output T_e is lower. In other words, the monopolist sells less, but at a higher price than companies in free competition.

Figure B.3 presents the equilibrium that is reached when a monopolist has U-shape costs and linear demand.

Now let us return to the issue of dwell time. We have demonstrated that, except for some specific cases where port storage is a cheaper option than private storage, longer port dwell time generally translates into higher total logistics costs. Higher port dwell time in figure B.3 would shift the MC curve upward.

The new equilibrium price that would optimize profits of the monopolist firm would therefore be superior to p_e and the corresponding output level, T_e, would be lower. In short, the company facing longer dwell times would sell even fewer units, but at an even higher price. This is evident in the trade of consumer goods in the countries under consideration (low demand and high prices).

But we can demonstrate analytically that, in general, this results in a net loss for the monopolist company because the higher price does not make up for the lost sales (in figure B.4, the darker π_2 section is smaller than initial profits π_1).

Therefore, a rational monopolist that charges the profit-maximizing price will seek to reduce port dwell times to optimize profits. However, other pricing behaviors of monopolist companies seem to contradict this conclusion.

A few traders operating in monopolistic situations, especially in land-locked countries, set their prices such that their profits are not affected by adverse logistics conditions, such as delays in delivery and congestion in ports. They just calculate their total logistics costs for each operation after delivery and apply a constant markup to set the final selling price (cost-plus strategy). These traders seem to be indifferent to longer dwell times because their margins and profits are unaffected and they pass on to their customers any extra logistics costs due to longer dwell time.

However, if we try to project this situation, we reach a different conclusion: higher marginal costs would normally lead to a different monopoly

Figure B.4   Translation of Monopoly Equilibrium and Profit Variation in the Scenario of Higher Dwell Time

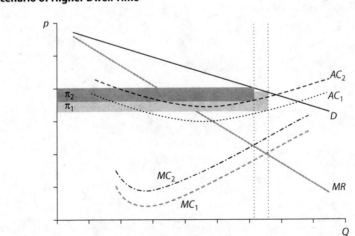

Source: Authors.
Note: AC_1 = initial average cost; AC_2 = average cost in the scenario of a higher dwell time; D = demand; MC_1 = initial marginal cost; MC_2 = marginal cost in the scenario of a higher dwell time; p = price; Q = output; π_1 = initial profits; π_2 = profits in the scenario of a higher dwell time.

equilibrium, with a higher selling price, but also lost sales. If the company manages to keep its total profits unaffected by a price rise, the demand curve will be different from the one depicted in figure B.4.

In this case, we have a situation close to the one depicted in figure B.5, where demand is inelastic to price, at least for reasonable price variations. Very desirable products, such as critical production inputs or indispensable food supplies or drugs, perhaps would be purchased by customers at any price, unless their price reaches unaffordable levels or becomes so high that the customer would bear the consequences of not buying the product. We can represent demand in this context by a vertical line or a kinked curve of the kind shown in figure B.5.

Demand for product Y is normally equal to T_e in this scenario, which would be, for example, the total number of people affected by a given disease every year who absolutely need to purchase medication. However, if the price reaches a superior boundary p_1, some of these patients will not be able to afford this medication and will not purchase it. If the price is as cheap as p_2, some healthy people will rush to purchase the drug at this competitive price, either to use it or to resell it later. In between these two boundaries, all normal users will be willing to purchase the drug, regardless of the price. The monopolistic traders choose to apply a constant

Figure B.5   Monopoly Equilibrium with a Kinked Demand Curve (Inelastic Demand between Two Price Boundaries p_1–p_2)

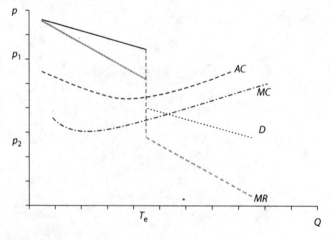

Source: Authors.
Note: AC = average cost; D = demand; MC = marginal cost; MR = marginal revenue; p = price; p_1 = superior price boundary; p_2 = inferior price boundary; Q = output; T_e = annual level of output.

markup to keep their profits unaffected, even in the case of higher total logistic costs.

In figure B.6, the darker π_2 section is equal to initial profits, π_1, despite the net increase in average cost. In addition, in this case the cost-plus pricing strategy is not the profit-maximizing strategy (a price of p_1 would optimize profits in both cases). But it might be a better strategy in the long term, because charging the maximum price, p_1, to all customers willing to pay a price between p_2 and p_1 might lead to a significant amount of lost sales if market demand evolves toward a continuous demand curve between the two price segments observed. Said differently, the inelastic demand function observed here is very likely to be elastic in the long term, because customers would find substitutes. The monopolistic trader therefore prefers to raise his prices to reflect higher logistics costs but to lower the price when logistics costs fall again. However, it is socially impossible to charge very high prices for necessity goods, and a monopolist would therefore face social unrest and public regulation if he were to raise his prices to the profit-maximizing price in all situations.

The second conclusion is therefore that a monopolist who opts for a cost-plus pricing strategy when demand is inelastic to price will not be affected in the short term by higher logistics costs and will make no effort

Figure B.6   Translation of Monopoly Equilibrium and Profit Variation in the Scenario of Higher Dwell Time and Cost-Plus Pricing Strategy

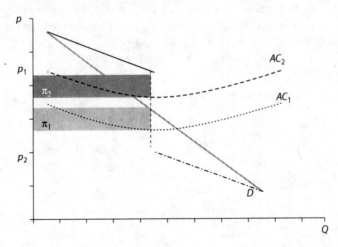

Source: Authors.
Note: AC_1 = initial average cost; AC_2 = average cost in the scenario of a higher dwell time; D = demand; p = price; p_1 = superior price boundary; p_2 = inferior price boundary; Q = output; π_1 = initial profits; π_2 = profits in the scenario of a higher dwell time.

to reduce dwell times in case of occasional congestion or occasional inefficiencies of port operators. Such a scenario is likely to happen for cyclical patterns of demand that are elastic to price only in the long term (food supplies, drugs, equipment).

A third pricing behavior derived from this situation of inelastic demand and observed among monopolistic companies is opportunistic pricing. Such traders use, for example, the pretext of higher logistics costs to increase substantially their selling prices. It is especially the case for category C (traders from landlocked countries) during rainy seasons or port congestion periods. For example, a 10 to 20 percent increase in total logistics costs might translate into a 30 percent increase in price. If we refer back to figure B.6, traders would charge price p_2 as soon as any difficulty is noticed in the port or along the transport corridor.

Another example of opportunistic behavior is when shippers prefer leaving their cargo in the port until the price peaks in an upward season. They create an artificial shortage in the local market and delay early deliveries until market prices rise. For example, in a situation similar to the one depicted in figure B.7, deliveries will be postponed for at least six or seven days. This is a very particular situation, where rising costs do not constitute a sufficient incentive to accelerate the clearance of goods because expected profits more than balance the extra costs.

Uncertainty about future profits or market risks generally leads traders to behave on the basis of expected expenses and returns rather than absolute levels. The three pricing strategies just discussed (monopoly equilibrium pricing, cost-plus pricing, and opportunistic pricing) are thus complemented by an analysis of expected profits and costs in the next section.

Figure B.7   Price Hike in a Shortage Situation

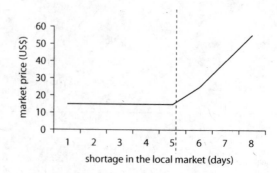

Source: Authors.

Regulation and market controls such as import quotas, price ceilings and floors, or taxation tools also affect pricing decisions of monopolists.

Pricing Strategies of Oligopolies

Oligopolies are situations in which a few firms account for the totality of the sales of product Y. Although economic theory generally leaves the oligopoly situation aside and starts by studying the theoretical aspects of free competition and monopolies, the prevalent competitive context of most market segments, especially in Sub-Saharan African countries, is arguably the oligopolistic context.

In this context, firms cannot neglect the market power of competitors, which is negligible in both the competitive and monopolistic situations. Price is affected by the moves of other firms and is not exogenous, and some competitors have a non-negligible size in relation to the total size of the market, which gives them substantial market power.

This distribution of market power in the hands of a few firms can lead to several typical situations and strategies, and economists generally distinguish between the following ones:

- Cartels
- Leader-followers
- Price war (Bertrand competition)
- Nash equilibria–Cournot competition
- Kinked oligolopy

Cartels and leader-followers. Cartels act as a virtual monopolist company: market players agree on prices so that they maximize profits in a consensual manner. In leader-follower situations, a single company, usually the biggest market player, imposes its pricing strategy on the other market players, who avoid any competitive move that would upset the leader. In short, the leader acts as a virtual monopolist, and followers are subject to its pricing strategy. This first two oligopolistic situations therefore lead to situations comparable to the monopolistic situation:

- It is in the general interest of profit-maximizing firms to reduce dwell times.
- In particular situations with inelastic demand, higher costs might have no noticeable impact on profit levels, and traders will be indifferent to higher dwell times.

- Opportunistic pricing strategies are used occasionally by traders to charge higher prices and increase their profits, despite longer dwell times and higher logistics costs.

Price war. Price war is the particular consequence of a duopolistic or oligopolistic situation where firms refuse to cooperate and favor short-run selfish interests. Firms act as price takers and compete by setting prices simultaneously so that the competitive equilibrium is reached despite the limited number of firms. In this context, companies end up pricing goods at marginal cost, and higher dwell time simply translates into higher marginal costs but does not affect the competitive equilibrium: all companies try to reduce dwell time and logistics costs to optimize profits. This is sometimes observed in the trade of second-hand products such as fabrics, electronics, and cars, where some companies are as efficient in terms of cargo clearance time as the largest companies operating in the market, simply because they are trying to win any marginal competitive advantage over their few competitors.

Nash equilibrium. A third interesting situation in which firms try to optimize their profits given the decision of other players leads to what is known as Nash equilibrium. It is the most documented scenario and has been deeply analyzed using the powerful body of knowledge of game theory. There is a large set of possible strategies, including collusion, Cournot pricing, or good-faith behavior, but the most important conclusion for our analysis is that cooperative behaviors are generally preferred because they are most profitable for all players.

We are interested here in possible reactions to rising total logistics costs as a consequence of higher dwell times. We can expect in this context that cooperative pricing strategies will not challenge existing price equilibriums and will lead either to limited price adjustments to outweigh additional costs or to relatively stable prices to avoid the risk of lost sales.

Kinked oligopoly. Finally, the interesting kinked demand curve theory also helps to explain why prices are quite stable in oligopolistic situations and why discrete price adjustments are more frequent than continuous variations. The fear of the unpredictable consequences of price changes is instrumental in discouraging the few players to undertake any disequilibrating price move. Short-term variations are seldom envisaged, and there is a threshold phenomenon where all companies keep prices stable despite variable logistics costs. This is observed in the consumer goods industry, where clients know prices because of advertising, and companies do not risk destabilizing the market even if they face higher logistics costs as a result of port congestion, for example.

The Issue of Uncertainty and Its Impact on Profits

In the first section of this appendix, we present a cost-minimization model that leads to alternative strategies of operators who do and do not possess private storage facilities. These strategies explain the behavior of operators who generally intend to minimize the dwell time of their containers in port, except when they face cash constraints or prohibitive financial costs.

To construct the model, we make a very strong assumption that traders have a perfect certainty about market demand and dwell times. We relax this assumption here and address the impact of uncertainty from an inventory management perspective. Uncertainty also affects revenues to a larger extent because of the possible impact on prices and thus revenues. We then address the issue of expected revenues and profits. We show that taking uncertainty into account does not change the dynamics of cost minimization or profit maximization; it actually strengthens the conclusions stated at the start of this appendix.

Inventory Management and the Issue of Safety Stocks

We have assumed that transit times and demand forecasts are perfectly predictable. This is a strong assumption that does not match reality. In practice, shippers hold an extra amount of stock, known as safety stock, that both covers risks and helps to prevent a shortage of stock in case of congestion, damage during transit, or unanticipated peak in demand.

There is a large set of inventory management practices, and proper dimensioning of safety stock is a painstaking task, especially for unreliable supply chains. The trade-off is to try and reduce, on the one hand, the level of safety stock to keep inventory costs low, but to have, on the other hand, enough extra stock to buffer against stockouts if actual demand exceeds expected demand, for example.

Let us calculate safety stock for these occurrences first—that is, demand forecast errors. A commonly used safety stock calculation is as follows: Safety stock = service factor $\times$ standard deviation of demand $\times$ lead time$^{1/2}$. For example, the service factor is 1.64 at the 95 percent satisfaction level, if we assume normal distribution of errors in demand forecast.

Standard deviation of demand should be estimated using approximated distribution based on empirical values. Let us assume, for example, that yearly demand of commodity Y is well approximated by a Poisson process of parameter T. The standard deviation in this case is $T^{1/2}$.

Different formulas are used for dwell time, depending on the shipper's aversion to risk (maximum lead time, minimum lead time, median value). In this case, we consider that the shipper has no ability to reorder during interval s. The maximum lead time in case of shortage is therefore the interval between two replenishments plus total transit time: lead time = $s + t_m + t_p + t_i$.

We, therefore, get the following formula for safety stock, SL, corresponding to an error in demand forecasts only:

$$SL = 1.64\sqrt{T}\sqrt{s + t_m + t_p + t_i}\,. \tag{B.13}$$

The safety stock corresponding to errors in forecast and uncertainty of transit time is given by a more developed formula:

Safety stock = service factor × (average lead time ×
standard deviation of demand² + standard deviation
of lead time² × average demand).$^{1/2}$ $\qquad$ (B.14)

The first term corresponds to shortages because of an error in forecast, while the second corresponds to shortages because of an uncertainty in lead times.

If we keep the same assumption of normal distribution of errors and Poisson processes (for both demand and transit times), we get the following:

$$SL = 1.64\sqrt{2T(s + t_m + t_p + t_i)}\,. \tag{B.15}$$

If we add the latter expression of safety stock level to the average stock in process $Ts/2$, we get a new average stock level:

$$i = \frac{Ts}{2} + 1.64\sqrt{2T(s + t_m + t_p + t_i)}. \tag{B.16}$$

For example, if we set

Annual quantity imported, T = 200 TEUs
Interval between reorders, s = 90 days
Maritime transit time, t_m = 15 days

Port dwell time, t_p = 25 days
Inland transit time, t_i = 5 days,

we get an average stock level i = 45 TEUs, decomposed into 25 TEUs of strategic inventory and 20 TEUs of safety stock.

This stock is split between inventory inside the port storage facilities and inventory in private storage facilities. The previous conclusion on the arbitrage between both storage options is still valid: potential savings in inventory holding costs should outweigh financial costs to justify early clearance of cargo from the port.

The new total logistics cost becomes, however, nonlinear in s and is thus no longer solvable analytically. Because the average stock level is more important here than in the simplified case of perfect certainty, the conclusions on the relationship between port dwell time and reorder interval or total cost are still valid:

- A longer dwell time inevitably hampers the supply chain by increasing the immobilization cost, and shippers react by having more frequent deliveries of materials (s diminishes).
- A longer dwell time severely affects total logistics costs because of the additional storage and depreciation costs.

The Impact of Uncertainty on Revenues and Profits
We have defined two kinds of uncertainty: uncertainty attached to errors in demand forecasts and uncertainty in delivery times. Both uncertainties adversely affect total logistics costs because they induce higher inventory levels and thus higher storage costs and depreciation costs.

If we look at profit maximization rather than cost minimization alone, both uncertainties have a further impact. Uncertainty attached to delivery times has an impact on revenues if we consider the negative impact of late shipments. In general terms, late shipments induce customer dissatisfaction and the possibility of lost sales (if the customer turns to another supplier or cancels his order) of the kind depicted by the solid line in figure B.8. If shipment arrival is not deterministic but follows some probabilistic distribution, the revenue profile becomes of the kind depicted in the dashed line because of the uncertainty of lead times. There are extra losses due to uncertainty since the customer will turn more rapidly to other sources of supply than in deterministic scenarios, and prices will fall more rapidly in the event of logistics congestion. In conclusion, uncertainty affects both revenues and profits in a negative way.

Figure B.8   Uncertain Delivery Times and Revenue

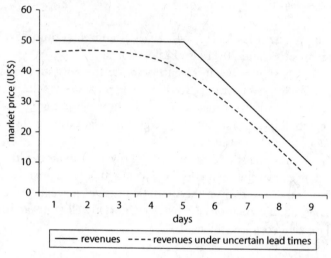

Source: Authors.

Uncertainty in demand forecasts also leads to uncertainty in expected revenues due to the direct relation between revenue and sales. With expected values of the demand distribution being lower than the corresponding deterministic demand because of uncertainty, revenues are, in general, lower if there is some risk of errors in forecasts.

Risks attached to any attribute (maritime transit time, dwell time, total sales) of the profit function lead to probabilistic formulations that generally have an adverse impact on absolute profit levels but do not change the strategies of market players. In a comfortable price-setting scenario, experience suggests that market players tend to be overcautious and to "build delay time into their production planning" to prepare for the worst situation. If the container happens to arrive on time, they just delay the shipment until they need it (Wood et al. 2002, 169). This hedging behavior is therefore another justification of why "shippers are biased in favor of utilizing the port facility as much as possible" (UNCTAD 1995).

Notes

1. Typical value for t_1 is less than one day, while t_2 and t_3 have typical values of five to 40 days.

2. In practice, all shippers can be grouped into one of the two categories according to the importance of port and warehouse storage time.

References

Magala, Mateus, and Adrian Sammons. 2008. "A New Approach to Port Choice Modeling." *Maritime Economics and Logistics* 10 (1–2): 9–34.

Quandt, R. E., and W. J. Baumol. 1969. "The Demand for Abstract Transport Modes: Some Hopes." *Journal of Regional Science* 9 (1): 159–62.

Rodrigue, Jean-Paul, and Theo Notteboom. 2009. "The Terminalization of Supply Chains: Reassessing Port-Hinterland Logistical Relationships." *Maritime Policy and Management* 36 (2): 165–83.

UNCTAD (United Nations Conference on Trade and Development). 1995. *Strategic Port Pricing.* UNCTAD/SDD/PORT2. New York: UNCTAD.

Wood, Donald F., Anthony P. Barone, Paul R. Murphy, and Daniel L. Wardlow. 2002. *International Logistics,* 2d ed. San Francisco: AMACOM Books.

Main Descriptive Statistics of Firm Surveys

Figure C.1   Main Activity of Importers

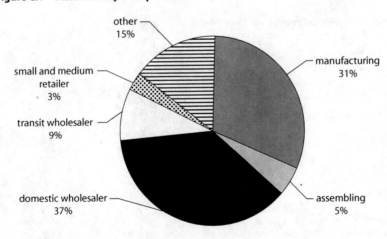

Source: World Bank firm surveys.
Note: The percentage is the share of each category in the total number of firm surveys.

Figure C.2   Annual Volume of Imports

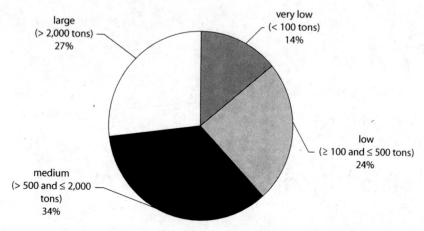

Source: World Bank firm surveys.
Note: The percentage is the share of each category in the total number of firm surveys.

Figure C.3   Annual Frequency of Deliveries

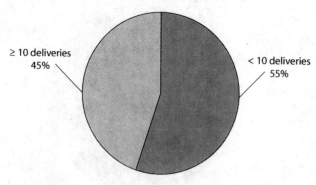

Source: World Bank firm surveys.
Note: The percentage is the share of each category in the total number of firm surveys.

Figure C.4   Degree of Competition among Importers

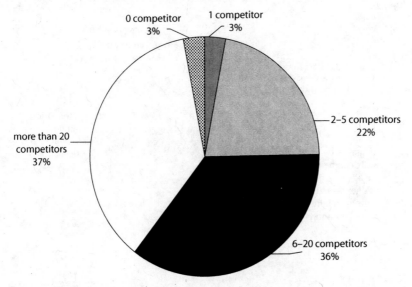

Source: World Bank firm surveys.
Note: The percentage is the share of each category in the total number of firm surveys.

Figure C.5   Monopoly-Oligopoly and Competition among Importers

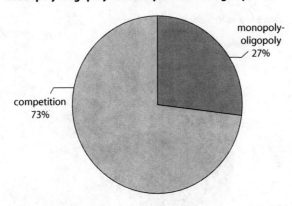

Source: World Bank firm surveys.
Note: The percentage is the share of each category in the total number of firm surveys.

Figure C.6   Level of Information about the Clearance Process Provided by C&F Agents

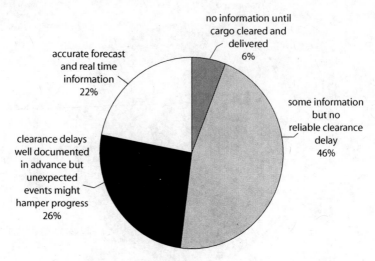

Source: World Bank firm surveys.
Note: The percentage is the share of each category in the total number of firm surveys.

Figure C.7   Main Factors in Selecting C&F Agents

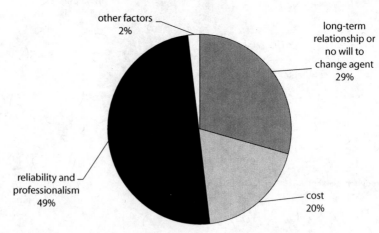

Source: World Bank firm surveys.
Note: The percentage is the share of each category in the total number of firm surveys.